HeartPrint

HeartPrint

UNLOCK THE WISDOM OF YOU

BY MEG TUOHEY

Copyright © 2026 by Meg Tuohey

All rights reserved. No part of this book may be used or reproduced in any manner whatsoever without prior written consent of the author, except as provided by the United States of America copyright law.

Published by Wisdom Stripes Press, St. Augustine, FL
Printed in the United States of America.

ISBN Hardcover: 979-8-9933570-1-0
ISBN Softcover: 979-8-9933570-0-3
ISBN eBook: 979-8-9933570-2-7

This publication is designed to provide accurate and authoritative information with regard to the subject matter covered. It is sold with the understanding that the publisher is not engaged in rendering legal, accounting, or other professional advice. If legal advice or other expert assistance is required, the services of a competent professional should be sought.

For more information, please write:
Wisdom Stripes Press
1775 US-1 No. 1070
St. Augustine, FL 32084

For Alfred, Tex, and Xander—the very best parts of my life

And for Buddy, Red, Luca, Ally, and Squirtle—faithful companions

Begin your own HeartPrint journey.

Visit

megantuohey.com/book

@megtuoheyofficial

Megan Tuohey - Making Relationships Work

@megtuoheyofficial

@megtuoheyofficial

The Wisdom Stripes Podcast

megantuohey.com/wisdom-stripes

Put your hand on your heart every morning and feel its beat.

It's your reminder that you're alive, that life is still choosing you.

Your heart is the most important muscle in your body; it works without pause … the most devoted rhythm you'll ever know.

Start there, in gratitude.

—Adriana Martin

The Invitation

Please Read This Part

Hello! My name is Meg, and I'm the author of this book. I am pleased to present this labor of love to you. It is the culmination of decades of work with myself and others. As with any good book, I hope you will laugh, cry, and be touched by it. I also hope to challenge and expand your thinking so that you yourself will grow as you track the journey of our two heroines.

Your HeartPrint

Let me start by discussing the title of the book, *HeartPrint*. I believe that each one of us was brought into this world with our own Heart-Print. Like fingerprints or DNA, it is unique. It is who we are meant to be. Here are some things that make up our HeartPrint.

- **Our Dreams.** Each of us has our own dreams. Yours might be to live on a farm and enjoy fresh milk each morning. Or it might be to reside in a bustling city with a lively social life. Whatever you are meant to be, it is a gift given to you, and it is meant to be honored.
- **Our Relationship Style.** Some HeartPrints are gregarious and people-centered, while others are more reclusive, focusing on intimate connections. Each of them is valuable in its own way.

- **Our Essence.** Maybe we like to go fast. Maybe we are slower and more deliberate. Perhaps we are attracted to the outdoors. Or, we might feel more at home in a well-appointed room.
- **Our Legacy.** This is what we make and create over our lifetime. When you reach the end of your life and you look back, will the way you've lived match who you are? Will your life have been coherent with your authentic essence?

When we are living in our HeartPrint, we have greater access to satisfaction, contentment, happiness, and fulfillment. Our life largely feels right, like things are in place, as though we are generally in sync with ourselves and the world around us. It's not that everything is perfect, because the human experience doesn't allow for this. It's more like we are able to locate who we truly are during the high and low points of our lives. And we are able to bring our unique and wise selves to whatever we might face.

Our HeartPrint never changes. It's who we were born to be. It grows and expands like a unique and beautiful plant, expressing itself differently as it matures, while the essence remains the same.

The challenge for all of us is that over time, it's easy to lose touch with our HeartPrint. We might have a hard time locating it during times of stress or mistreatment, or when trying to live up to others' expectations. So, we end up responding to life in ways that initially make us feel safe, and which ultimately keep us stuck. Then, we stop blooming as a person. It's like a vine wrapping itself around a beautiful tree and blocking the light and nutrients the tree needs to grow tall and strong. It's still the same tree, but it is malnourished by the vine and therefore can't be all that it was meant to be until it can emerge from the vine and claim its rightful place.

When we lose touch with our HeartPrint, we feel lost—disconnected at best, and helpless, hopeless, angry, and contemptuous at worst. It can sometimes feel like we are living someone else's version of our life. Pressure from society, expectations from family, and past emotional wounds shape the way we see ourselves, causing us to doubt, suppress our best selves, and stray from our truest path.

No matter how buried or obscured the relationship with our HeartPrint becomes, it never disappears. It is always there, waiting to be uncovered and embraced. It is the greatest journey of our lives.

So, this book is about discovering, rediscovering, and connecting with our HeartPrint—learning to listen to its whispers, honoring its wisdom, and allowing it to shine through in every aspect of our lives.

When we live in our HeartPrint, we don't just exist—we have the specific-to-us ingredients we need to thrive.

If you have lost hope about how good your life can feel, I want to give that back to you. Our HeartPrint is our essence. It's the center of who we are.

Your Wise Woman

One more thing I want to mention, and it's very important. We don't just have our innate HeartPrint. I believe that each of us also has someone I like to call your Wise Woman. She is that part of you who can guide you to your HeartPrint. She has full, direct access to who we truly are. She is our inner wisdom. She gently (and sometimes firmly) leads us to understand our HeartPrint.

She helps us to make decisions that lead us to live most of the time in our HeartPrint. My deep desire is for you and your Wise Woman to simply live the life you were meant to live. This life certainly has its share of troubles. But it's a life where you can show up most days as the best version of yourself. It's a life where you are connected, confident, and fulfilled.

Before we dive in, let me share about the fanciful format of the book. There are two main characters, Elizabeth and Ellie. They are actually the same person. Ellie is the growing and human part of Elizabeth, seeking to connect with her HeartPrint. We will watch her as she works throughout her life to first locate, then get close to, and finally live in her HeartPrint.

Elizabeth is Ellie's Wise Woman. She is the compass that constantly encourages Ellie to connect with and embrace her HeartPrint. Elizabeth will share with you, the reader, her insights and wisdom as we recount different scenes from throughout their shared life.

As you read, I would like to ask you to play along with me. Elizabeth is presented as Ellie's *fully formed* Wise Woman from the beginning of the book. I understand that that is a bit unfair to you because generally, your Wise Woman grows along with you. I did this to help you identify and connect with your own Wise Woman.

Our HeartPrint is the full expression of who we are meant to be. Our Wise Woman is the conduit for understanding, connecting, and living in coherence with our HeartPrint. She is the compass that guides us on our voyage.

Our Wise Woman is the voice inside that says things like, *This doesn't feel quite right,* and *I think we can do better than this,* and *We don't have to settle for a life like this.* It is a guiding voice that must be heeded.

I hope you have heard from your Wise Woman before. And, after reading this book, my wish is that you build a relationship with her, and that she becomes more and more a part of your daily life.

Your Wise Woman *might* sound like Elizabeth. She might not. But I know you have a voice like Elizabeth's that guides you to your HeartPrint—a life where you have greater access to fulfillment, connection, and satisfaction; a life which, when you look back on it, is one that is uniquely yours, where you understand that you lived your life being true to who you really are.

So, indulge me as I weave a little magic into the pages to come. I've written them with the hope that they may stir something true and life-giving within you. It's time to begin!

A Letter from Elizabeth

Hello, new friend,

I asked Meg if it would be okay if I wrote you a letter before you began reading the book. She happily agreed.

You and I will have a chance to talk throughout this book about the tender and beautiful journey of Ellie as she connects to and lives in her HeartPrint. And before we get started, I'd like to tell you a bit about myself. As you know, I'm Elizabeth. You'll meet Ellie (me) in Chapter 0. As Meg mentioned, we are one and the same person.

Crazy, right?

I am going to ask you to suspend your disbelief as you read. I know there will be parts of the story that just don't make sense from a logical standpoint. But thankfully, there's more to life than logic. For instance, I am writing this letter, as they say, posthumously. You see, I have already transitioned into the next part of life. But through the magic of the written word, I can do things like this. I think that is somewhat wonderful, don't you?

I also bring some interesting abilities to our party. At once, I'm able to see the past, the present, and the future, all at the same time. I can put the events of Ellie's life into perspective. I have the benefit of *wisdom* (which is why I'm called Ellie's Wise Woman!).

It took Ellie and me decades to fully connect. Your Wise Woman may feel somewhat distant from you. Rest assured, she is right there with you, ready for the journey toward your HeartPrint. I promise you that as you grow, you will hear her more clearly.

We are about to go on a profound journey that has many obstacles, tragedies, and triumphs. Besides Ellie and me, you'll meet some other characters along the way. First, there are Lisa and John, Ellie's parents. You'll be introduced to Grace, Ellie's lifelong friend. And then there's Joe, her husband, and Chase, her son. I think you'll love Miss Keene, Chase's teacher. I could go on, but I'm sure you're excited to get started.

The journey to live in your HeartPrint won't be a straight line. There will be setbacks. And there will be great victories and joyous moments along the way. It's a journey well worth taking. You'll see this mirrored within Ellie's story.

I want to share one more thought before we part ways for a few minutes. The goal of this book is for you to become great friends with your Wise Woman so that you can live in your HeartPrint.

Your Wise Woman is unique to you, and you alone. Her job is to help you live in your HeartPrint. You might currently have a strong relationship with your Wise Woman already. You might not know her at all. Maybe that connection has come and gone intermittently up until now. Perhaps you're connected by a thin strand, a moderate bond, or a strong, thriving relationship.

You might not even relate to what I'm talking about at all. This might be the beginning of you meeting your Wise Woman. Whatever your relationship with her is, it's okay. My dream is to see you build an even stronger connection with her. If you don't know your Wise Woman, I am happy to act as a stand-in for her, until you make the connection for yourself.

That would be a wonderful outcome.

Okay, enough about that. Let's see how Ellie started her journey. With warm love and admiration,

Contents

The First Part 1

    Chapter 0 • Age 0 3

    Chapter 1 • Age 10 13

    Chapter 2 • Age 17 23

    Chapter 3 • Age 28 35

    Chapter 4 • Age 31 47

    Chapter 5 • Age 33 53

    Chapter 6 • Age 41 63

The Second Part 75

    Chapter 7 • Age 42 79

    Chapter 8 • Age 43 85

    Chapter 9 • Age 43 99

    Chapter 10 • Age 43 115

    Chapter 11 • Age 43 129

    Chapter 12 • Age 43 145

    Chapter 13 • Age 44 161

Interlude 171

The Third Part 175

    Chapter 14 • Age 48 177

    Chapter 15 • Age 50 191

Chapter 16 • Age 52 205

Chapter 17 • Age 52 215

The Last Part..**221**

Chapter 18 • Age 63 223

Chapter 19 • Age 76 233

Chapter 20 • Age 89 241

Epilogue **247**

Acknowledgments **255**

About the Author **259**

The First Part

Awakening

Chapter 0 · Age 0

the delivery room at Vibra Hospital in Rochdale, Massachusetts—the story begins

The soul that would someday be called Ellie turned inside her mother's womb. Like every child born, she had her own distinctive HeartPrint. This child was given a spirit of adventure. She was meant to be strong, determined, and intense. She was intended to be protective, connected to animals, and full of curiosity. Her life was a canvas waiting to be painted with bold strokes of experience and wonder.

Though she couldn't understand the outside world around her, the past nine months had already begun the long arc of human experience that continually puts pressure on one's connection to their HeartPrint. Her father's angry shouts and her mother's stress quietly pulsed through her blood, leaving their subtle imprint on her beautiful brain and nervous system. Her parents' confusion and pain were being passed on to her, just like her father's height or her mother's eye color.

The time came for her to be born. The infant registered the pain of forceps pressing into her head. She couldn't understand phrases like "The mother is losing a lot of blood" or "Be ready to take this child to NICU." But somehow, the fear in the room found its way into her, inching her away from her HeartPrint.

After 15 hours of labor, Ellie came into the world, but she was swiftly separated from her mother, Lisa. Lisa lay on the bed, barely conscious. She was a petite woman who had struggled to deliver her nine-pound daughter. Drained from the ordeal and weakened by heavy blood loss, she slipped into a deep, exhausted sleep.

When Ellie's mother awoke, she instinctively reached for her stomach. She was confused by the emptiness where her swollen belly had been. She turned on her side and blankly stared out the window. A nurse soon entered, cradling Ellie, who had recovered with remarkable resilience, in her arms.

"Here's your daughter," the nurse said, smiling.

Lisa turned her head toward the nurse and child. She looked at the baby being offered to her and said, "That's not my baby," and turned away to continue gazing out the window.

The nurse's smile faltered. "Of course it is. You gave birth last night," she said, edging closer.

"That is not my baby," Lisa said emphatically. This time, she didn't even look around.

"Well," the nurse replied, "I'll take her back to the nursery for now. We can try again later."

Lisa said nothing and felt nothing.

The nurse left the room. She stopped outside the room where Lisa's husband, John, was sitting. He stood up, towering over the nurse.

"Mama is going through a hard time," she said, glancing back and forth between the tall man and the tiny baby. "I'll take this one back to the nursery for now. Hopefully, Mom will do better when she gets home. She's due to check out later today."

John couldn't make eye contact with the nurse. He stared at his daughter with a furrowed brow. He nodded his head and quietly muttered, "Yeah, sure." As Ellie was carried away, John took a deep breath and walked into the hospital room.

John and Lisa were dealing with much more than the birth of their daughter. Their relationship was strained to the point of breaking. During the sixth month of her pregnancy, Lisa had discovered that he had been unfaithful. Despite his pleas and promises, she was resolute in her anger, unwilling to discuss their future together.

"They said they're sending you home today," John said quietly from across the room. Lisa was still staring out the window and didn't respond.

"Your mom is coming over and staying a few days," he said, without emotion. "I'll be back to help a little later." John walked out of the room, leaving Lisa alone.

A few hours later, the nurses packed Lisa and Ellie into the car and they headed home. Lisa's mother was waiting on the doorstep as the car pulled into the driveway. John got out, opened the back seat door, and removed the infant from her car seat. Lisa, disheveled, weak, and in pain, opened the car door and slowly crawled out, paying no attention to Ellie. The baby's new grandmother, startled by her daughter's appearance, went to her first.

"My goodness," Lisa's mom said as she supported her daughter by holding onto her arm. "Let's get you inside."

As she helped Lisa, she noticed John carrying the new child. "She's beautiful!" she exclaimed, as she took Lisa's arm. "What is this precious child's name?"

"We are calling her Elizabeth," John said, showing a small smile.

"Elizabeth!" Lisa's mom repeated. "I cannot *wait* to meet you."

Lisa's mother helped her daughter into the house. "How do you feel, sweetheart?" she whispered as they walked toward the bedroom.

"Tired," was all Lisa could say.

"Well, I'm here as long as you need me. It's time for you to rest," she said as she helped her daughter into bed.

Grandma walked into the living room, where John had placed Ellie in the crib. "Elizabeth!" she said brightly, walking to the crib and finding the baby cooing. She picked her up and held her close.

"Don't you worry about a thing, John," Grandma said. "I've got this. You must be exhausted. Why don't you get some rest?"

John muttered his agreement and disappeared down the hall, where he plopped into the bed in the guest room. Grandma sat in the rocking chair and brought her first grandchild near to her face.

"Elizabeth, I *love* you," she said, touching the baby's nose when she said *love*. "And your Mom and Dad *love* you. And your Grandpa *loves* you and wishes he could be here." She touched the child's nose each time she said the word *love*.

"I think I'll call you Ellie," she said quietly.
"My beautiful Ellie."

From Elizabeth

What a start to Ellie's story. It was all so traumatic, not just for Ellie, but for her mother and father as well. I'm so thankful for Ellie's Grandma. In the midst of all the craziness, she gave Ellie love and stability.

As I look back on this birth, a word that comes to mind is *inauspicious*. Even before being born, a thread started that would affect Ellie's HeartPrint for decades.

Ellie's mother said, "That's not my baby." This non-recognition of her child as her own is a clue to Lisa's inner experience. The physical pain from her difficult childbirth and the emotional pain of the infidelity in her marriage likely contributed to how she responded.

What makes it worse is Ellie's mom would tell this story often as Ellie grew up. They would be at a gathering, and when the conversation turned to children or births, Lisa felt compelled to tell everyone what she had said about Ellie in the hospital. It was usually said lightheartedly, and Lisa would laugh. Each time Ellie heard it, the wound of being unseen, unknown, and unimportant reopened.

Have you ever thought about how each of us is beholden to those who came before us? And that they are beholden to those who came before them? We pass on not just things like eye color and hair color but emotions as well. There's even a scientific word for it: *epigenetics*. It means we can actually carry not just the physical genes of those who came before us; we can also carry their traumas and their triumphs. These can move us away from our relationship with our Wise Woman, making it more difficult to live in congruence with our HeartPrint and fully express who we were meant to be.

For some of us, the deck was stacked against us from the start. We have multiple strands of confusion and pain that need to be untangled. Maybe they were handed down genetically. Maybe there was a lot of drama and trauma in our family. Maybe it's the way we were raised. Whether we are aware of them or not, all of these have an impact on our ability to access our HeartPrint.

Even if we had a "good childhood," there are still things there. No parent is perfect. I'm not saying there aren't great parents—there are. I'm saying that even the best of them leave us with some pain and confusion. It turns out that there's just no way to get through this life without having someone mistreat us, ignore us, or treat us disrespectfully. When that happens, especially when we are young and vulnerable, it tends to obscure the connection to our HeartPrint.

You see, we all have a beautiful brain, which, among other things, seeks to protect us. When we are threatened, either physically or emotionally, our brain just doesn't like it and will do what it perceives is needed to help us.

These threats can show up as unanswered questions. We ask ourselves, sometimes unconsciously, "Why would someone who is supposed to love me, care for me, and nurture me treat me that way?" That kind of unanswered question becomes a thread in our lives that needs to be untangled.

In Ellie's case, her parents were going through a difficult time during her birth. Ellie didn't discover until years later that her dad had been unfaithful. That is not exactly the nurturing environment for growth and stability.

Eventually, with some guidance from Grandma and Grandpa, John and Lisa temporarily worked things out. They actually stayed together for 12 more years after Ellie was born, during which time her brother, James, was born. This separation and conflict affected the connection to her HeartPrint, even in the womb.

I do want to mention Ellie's dear grandmother. I don't know what Ellie would have done without her. She was what is called a *protective factor*. That is someone who allowed Ellie to have a soft place to land and be cherished. It seems to me that life provides us with supportive characters from unexpected places. In Ellie's case, even though her mother had a lot of things going on, her grandmother was a stable and encouraging presence in her life for many years. Maybe it was because Grandma was from a different generation, but her presence is still one of Ellie's most cherished memories.

I'd like to invite you to start discovering what questions you have about your confusion and pain. That's really the first step to living in your HeartPrint. If you don't know what questions you have, how can you ever begin to answer them? Even if we can't put words to it, our beautiful brain demands answers to these questions. Without them being brought to the front of our mind, our brain will unconsciously seek answers elsewhere, often looking in the wrong places.

Maybe you have noticed that you have certain patterns in your relationships, like always being attracted to a certain type of person. Or you might tend to demand attention when you feel a certain way. Or perhaps you sometimes feel a need to fix things. This might be your brain trying to get answers it doesn't yet have. It's trying to find its way back to your HeartPrint.

Often, instead of uncovering and facing these questions, we just bury the questions, pain, and confusion. That actually works for a while—until it doesn't. Sooner or later, though, we reach a tipping point where these questions must be addressed, or there are catastrophic consequences.

I can't speak to where you are in your journey toward your HeartPrint. Only you can do that. What I do know is that discovering these unanswered questions, pain, and confusion are vital steps. Only by facing them can you begin to heal, reclaim your HeartPrint, and step fully into the life you were meant to live.

Okay, that's enough for now. I'm going to invite Meg in for a bit, and then we'll get back to our story. We will fast-forward 10 years. I'll never forget the day Ellie rode her bicycle to school for the first time. It was both triumphant and terrifying.

A Cup of Tea with Meg

We covered some important and foundational topics in this chapter. To locate and live in your HeartPrint, it's helpful to identify the generational challenges you might be facing. Here are some questions that can help:

- Would you say that you had a "good childhood"? Why or why not?
- Can you identify any significant moments in your childhood that feel unresolved?
- What did those experiences teach you? Maybe that you were unlovable, or untrustworthy, or you needed to be overly responsible? Maybe it was something totally different.
- How did those incidents affect the way you see yourself? And how did they shape your future interactions with your Loved Ones?

Chapter 1 · Age 10

on and off a Huffy bike in Sturbridge, Massachusetts—early lessons

"Slow down, Ellie!"

Ellie had no intention of slowing down. She was on her new bike, streamers flapping in the wind, her pigtails flying behind her as she coasted down a long, gentle slope. She had struggled to come up the hill on her way to school. Now was the fun part.

Her classmates whizzed by in her peripheral vision. *I must be going 100 miles an hour!* she thought. She grinned as she calculated how much sooner she would arrive home, which was just a few pedals past the bottom of the hill. She coasted with her feet off the pedals. She had never felt so free.

At the bottom of the hill, she had to make a quick maneuver to get off the road and onto the sidewalk to her house. That's when it happened. Instead of going up the driveway entrance, she clipped the sidewalk. Her bike stopped, but she kept going. She flew over the top of the handlebars, sailed past the sidewalk, and fell onto the ground. She landed on her chest and had the wind knocked out of her. She rolled over, unable to breathe.

She panicked, while trying to draw a breath. Shockingly, no air was coming in. Was she going to die? Why couldn't she breathe? She heard her neighbor shout, "Ellie, are you okay?" And then the neighbor called for Ellie's mother even louder. "Lisa! Ellie fell!" Lisa came outside and walked toward her daughter.

Ellie still couldn't catch her breath. She was panicked and distraught, believing that she would die right then and there. By the time her mother arrived at her side, Ellie was finally able to take some small breaths. Lisa kneeled next to her. "You've just had the breath knocked out of you," she said. "Does anything else hurt?"

Ellie's breathing slowly returned. "I couldn't breathe," she gasped quietly.

"Yes, you had the breath knocked out of you," her mother repeated unemotionally. "Does it hurt anywhere else?" Ellie pointed at her scraped knee.

"Let's get you up," Lisa said, placing her hands on Ellie's back. Ellie sat up. Yes, her knee did hurt. She stood up with the help of her mother. She saw her bike lying on the ground with the front wheel popped.

"Don't worry," the now-nearby neighbor said. "I'll get the bike."

Lisa helped Ellie walk the few steps to their house and had her lie down on the couch. She put some ice on the injured knee. "You got going a little fast, huh?" she asked.

Ellie didn't reply. She had gone from feeling complete freedom to thinking she was going to die in a matter of seconds. She didn't understand what her mom meant by her having had the breath knocked out of her. It was terrifying.

The dinner conversation that night included her brother, James, talking about his baseball game. Ellie's bike crash came up, and her dad promised to fix the wheel. "How's your knee, darlin'?" her dad asked.

"It hurts," Ellie said.

"Well, let's keep an eye on it for the next few days. You'll be good as new before you know it."

It was the last thing either of her parents said about the incident. That night, she crawled into bed and hugged Mama Bunny, her large, worn-out stuffed animal. The gift from her mother at the age of seven had gotten Ellie through many tough nights. It provided Ellie with physical comfort: It was big enough for nearly a full-body hug, soft and hard in all the right places, and a bit furry and a bit smooth. "Mama Bunny," she said quietly as she wrapped her torso around the stuffed animal, "You won't believe what happened today. I got the wind knocked out of me. It was very scary."

Mama Bunny listened attentively, as she always did.

"I guess I can't go so fast," Ellie said as she fell asleep.

"Mama Bunny," she whispered,
"you won't believe what happened today."

From Elizabeth

I still shudder when I think about that day. Ellie truly thought she was going to die. If you've ever had the wind knocked out of you, you know what I mean. Imagine it happening for the first time, and I think you'll understand how she felt.

The fall from the bike and what happened afterward show how questions, pain, and confusion can compound. It's like having open browser tabs on your computer. I'm not a techie, but I know that when I have 28 browser tabs open at the same time, my computer slows down. I understand it has something to do with the resources available.

The emotional trauma Ellie had when she was born can be represented by one of those open browser tabs. It required some of her resources. The thing is, that tab of the story of her birth and her mom saying "That's not my baby" stayed open. As time went on, other things came up in her life. She heard her mom and dad fight nastily (browser tab open). She saw her dad treat her brother differently from her (browser tab open). Her mom wasn't home when Ellie came home from school, and she had to make sure James did his homework when she herself needed help with her own homework (browser tab open).

The more open tabs we have, the more resources we need. It can become overwhelming to our brains. We learn how to cope with them the best we can, but it turns out that we end up with little or no energy to address the questions, pain, and confusion in our lives. Everything becomes more about survival.

Unfortunately, not only was Lisa, Ellie's mom, unable to help Ellie close any of those browser tabs, but she was also unable to see that Ellie was struggling. Lisa had plenty of open tabs herself. It took all the energy she had to negotiate her life. She was just trying to make it through each day.

In the absence of Lisa helping Ellie understand what happened with the bike, Ellie's beautiful brain had to figure it out herself. So, she reasoned out a rule for herself at the age of 10: "When I feel the freedom of flying down a hill, it might mean I could die." It was just that simple. She couldn't put it into words, but that's what she thought.

The bike wreck connected the feeling of *freedom* with the feeling of *danger*. This became a very strong connection for Ellie. She tried to express her feelings in her 10-year-old way, but they were understandably dismissed by her parents, who told her the danger wasn't real.

This raised questions in Ellie's mind that went beyond words. Unconsciously, she asked herself things like, *Can I be a person who enjoys freedom?* and *Who will take care of me when my life is in danger?* and *How can I make sense of all of this?* These are the open browser tabs just from this one incident.

Mama Bunny was a cherished part of Ellie's life. She comforted her the best she could. At least Ellie could talk to her. The problem was that Mama Bunny couldn't answer back.

So, how might Ellie have closed these open tabs? All it would have taken was a simple, connected conversation with her mom or dad. It may have sounded something like this:

Mom: "What was it like to fall off your bike and have the wind knocked out of you?"

Ellie: "It was *very* scary. I thought I was going to die."

Mom: "That must have been terrifying, sweetheart."

Ellie: "It was. And I was all by myself. I couldn't breathe. I guess I shouldn't have been going so fast."

Mom: "Ugh. I wish that hadn't happened to you. What was it like coming down the hill, though?"

Ellie (smiling): "It was so much fun! I was going, like, 100 miles an hour! I liked it."

Mom: "That does sound like fun. I like this part of you. You love to go fast. Don't stop that. I bet you've learned something about curbs, though." (smiling) "But don't stop going fast, sweetheart. It's who you are. Just take it easy sometimes. I remember when I was about your age and had the breath knocked out of me on the playground. I remember how scary it was. It's just something that happens sometimes. The next time you'll understand, and you'll know that small breaths through your nose will help inflate your lungs. I hope you won't be as scared."

With a conversation like that, Ellie's young brain would have processed her questions, pain, and confusion around the event. She would have understood the physiology of what happened. She would have learned to separate freedom from danger. It would have made Ellie wiser without robbing her of one of our great joys in life—the feeling of unrestrained freedom.

Ellie would have worked out why her body felt the way it did and why her emotions came up the way they did. She would have gotten what she needed for her brain to make sense of the experience. It all would have been integrated and organized. Ellie would have learned how to feel the thrill of going fast in a safe and organized way. That browser tab would have been closed, and she would have had more resources to apply to her other questions.

Unfortunately, all Ellie learned was simply, "I can't go fast."

You see, Ellie's HeartPrint included a joyful love of going fast. It was something she was born with. Sadly, on that day, Ellie began to unconsciously doubt her connection to that part of her HeartPrint. Without knowing it, she blocked out a part of the connection she and I had. She began to believe her human experience rather than trust her HeartPrint.

Regrettably, that is a very normal thing in life. To a greater or lesser extent, I feel certain this has happened to you in one way or another. You've had a human experience that pushed you away from your HeartPrint. These experiences cast a shadow on who you are and shrink the connection to your Wise Woman. It's understandable. From the available information Ellie had at the tender age of 10, it made sense that she simplified this into a rule that going fast was not good for her.

This would be a weighty belief Ellie would carry for many years before she was able to process it and therefore organize it in her mind. It wasn't inevitable that the incident would change her, but it did. Ellie could have just learned to watch for curbs. Instead, she decided there should be no more going fast. She had to play it safe.

Ellie's mom, Lisa, did not have "going fast" as a part of her HeartPrint. So it was hard for her to understand someone who did. She didn't know how to help. As I said earlier, everyone's HeartPrint is different. Recognizing and respecting those differences is a part of wisdom.

I'm wondering about your browser tabs, my HeartPrint friend. Have you ever thought about something like this? Maybe you can reel off several similar experiences off the top of your head. Maybe you find this difficult to relate to. Certainly, all of us have at least a few, right?

I hope it's encouraging to know that you have your very own Wise Woman who can help you with them. Let's discuss how we can connect you with her.

The first step is to *externalize* the feelings, confusion, and pain, like the imaginary conversation with Ellie's wise mother. That means either speaking them out loud or writing them down. Once they are out there in the open, we can begin to go deeper. Ellie won't be able to do this for quite some time in this story, but you can! The sooner it can happen for you, the better. See the drawing to help.

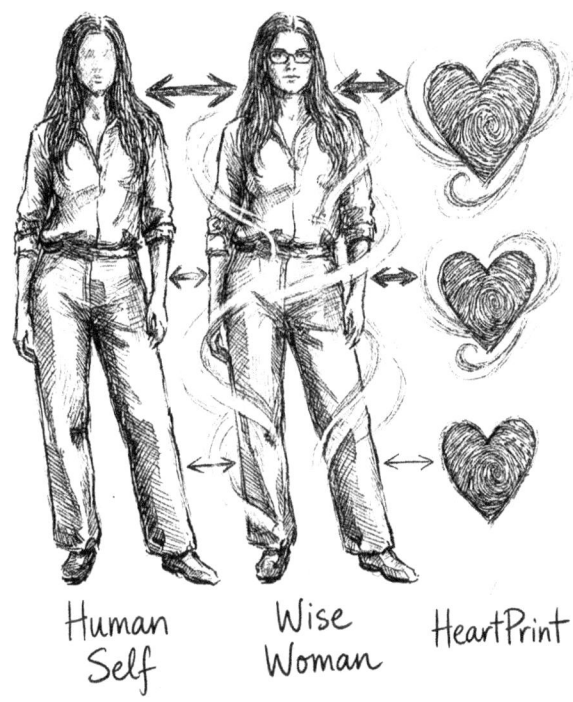

Your Wise Woman connects your human self to your HeartPrint, who is the person you were created to be.

First, you have your human self. It experiences life with all of its trouble, trauma, pain, and confusion. Then there's your Wise Woman. She is like a guide who connects you to your HeartPrint. And then there's your actual HeartPrint, which encompasses all the possibilities of who you were meant to be. The stronger your connection to your Wise Woman, the greater your access to your HeartPrint. Your Wise Woman is like a compass or a guide who helps you discover, explore, and live in your HeartPrint.

Well, back to our story. I wish I had good news to share. But over the next few years, things got more and more difficult for Ellie. At the age of 12, her parents divorced. Ellie and her brother, James, were shuffled back and forth between homes. Their dad was preoccupied with his job and didn't spend much time with them. Their mom had a steady stream of new boyfriends who were difficult to negotiate. More browser tabs just kept getting opened as Ellie drifted further and further from her Wise Woman and her HeartPrint.

When Ellie went to high school, she met her best friend, Grace. Although Grace's HeartPrint was completely different from Ellie's, they were "muy simpático." It's that way, isn't it? Have you ever noticed how certain people just feel comfortable to you? Their spirit somehow resonates with yours in an unspoken, real way. That's the way it was with Grace and Ellie.

Grace would become an integral part of Ellie's life. In high school, Grace had a crazy idea that forced Ellie into a big decision. She really needed some help working things through. And it was there, near a cabin, that Ellie and I first magically met.

A Cup of Tea with Meg

This chapter is all about unanswered questions. Some of the life events that happen in our childhood just never get resolved. And when they don't, they leave us with questions to answer as we become adults. Here are some ideas for your consideration:

- Did you have someone to talk to as a child who was accepting and accessible? Could they really see your unique self? What impact did that have on you?
- If we could send someone back in time to help you process your questions, confusion, and pain, what part of your timeline would you send them to first? What difference might that make?

Chapter 2 · Age 17

a basic cabin near Fiskdale, Massachusetts—first glimpse of Elizabeth

Somewhat unkempt, Ellie walked into her first-period precalculus class for juniors on Monday morning. She had spent the weekend at her father's house, where she never slept well.

Ellie had done her best to navigate her confusing childhood. There was the divorce, her mother's frequent trips, her father's constant moving, and her brother James's issues. Where Ellie had learned to be quiet, get along, and focus on school, James had a different reaction to the challenges. He had trouble focusing and would often have emotional outbursts at school and home.

For the first 12 years of her life, Ellie had at least known the stability of one home and two parents. Now, life had turned into a weekly game of musical beds. She had to cope with an unstable environment where her parents were continually bringing home new partners, and she was constantly feeling off-balance. She and James were forced to do adult things, like remembering what to pack, and when. They had to learn how to cope with the revolving door of different adults in their lives, and a schedule that changed every week. Although they had a roof over their heads, they didn't have anywhere that truly felt like home.

Ellie found comfort in the regularity of school. Although she considered herself "not so smart," she made up for it by working very hard. She had already decided to attend Northeastern University and study pharmacology.

"Hey, Elles," her friend Grace said as Ellie slid into her desk.

"Hey," Ellie said, brushing her blonde hair back with her hands.

Grace was Ellie's best friend. She was ambitious like Ellie. While Ellie was solidly middle-class, Grace's family had money. She had her own car and her parents lived in Fiskdale, the "nice part of town." They became friends as freshmen and bonded over Toni Braxton, Jim Carrey, and lacrosse. Both of them lamented their situations at home and their parents, who "just didn't get them."

"Rough weekend?" Grace asked, looking at Ellie's barely combed hair.

Ellie rolled her eyes. "Just another *Weekend at Bernie's*," she said, referencing one of their favorite old-time movies where a dead boss is propped up and presented as alive by two of his young employees.

Grace giggled. "I've got a surprise for you after school," she whispered, putting her finger over her lips. The teacher began his lesson.

"What is it?" Ellie whispered.

Grace shushed her and pointed to the teacher. Class began.

After school, Ellie walked to Grace's car for her ride home. "C'mon, let's go!" Grace said excitedly as Ellie slid into the front seat.

"What's the big surprise?" Ellie asked.

"I've got something you *have to see*," Grace said as she sped out of the parking lot and turned up "Un-Break My Heart" on the CD player.

"Where are you taking me?" Ellie asked as they got onto the ramp for Interstate 84.

Grace smiled. "You're going to have to wait. But you are going to *love* it."

Ten minutes later, Grace pulled off the freeway and drove down a quiet country road. She turned onto a dirt road, drove about a half mile, and parked in front of a modest cabin. It was weathered but well-kept, with three steps leading to a simple porch.

"Ta-da!" Grace said, holding both of her hands out toward the cabin.

"What is this place?" Ellie asked.

"It's mine!"

"It's yours?"

"It's all mine!" Grace exclaimed. "My uncle gave it to me. He said he never uses it. Well, I don't own it, but he said I can use it whenever I want. He's rich, and he never comes to Sturbridge. I mean, the cabin isn't that great ... yet. I want to move in here. And I want you to move in with me. We can both live here and finish school. No more *Weekend at Bernie's* for you, and no more of my dad for me. It's perfect! What do you say?"

Ellie looked at the cabin. Then she looked at Grace. "You want *us* to live *here* by *ourselves*?" she asked.

"Exactly. Think about it. We can drive to school together. Then we can come back here. Isn't it the *perfect* plan? C'mon. Check it out."

Before Ellie could say anything else, Grace was out of the car, up the steps, and unlocking the front door. Ellie followed, first stepping onto the porch and then inside. The cabin was a single room with plain furnishings and a faint musty smell, like a place that hadn't been lived in for a while. It wasn't dirty, just a little tired.

"We can share a bed," Grace said, pointing at a large bed on the far side of the cabin. "And here's the kitchen. And *look* what's out back." She opened the back door, and Ellie heard the rushing of water.

"It's a beautiful creek!" she said. "It'll be just you and me. You can study as much as you want. You won't have to stay at your dad's place anymore. It will be just *perfect*," she said, sighing. "What do you say?"

Ellie's head was spinning. This felt dangerous. "Your dad is okay with this?" Ellie asked.

"Well, I haven't exactly told him. But I don't care what he says. *I'm doing it.*"

"I don't think my mom would allow this," Ellie said.

"Oh, Elles," Grace said with disappointment. "You can't live your life for your mom. She's crazy. You told me that already. And I know how you feel about your dad."

Ellie allowed herself to think about this seemingly simple solution to her life. No more moving around. No more negotiating with the boyfriends and girlfriends of her parents. She could study. And she loved Grace, someone who was steady in her topsy-turvy world.

Then she thought about her brother, James. How could she leave him? What would happen to him if she weren't there to play referee between him and their parents? What would it be like for him if she weren't there anymore? Her ever-practical mind, honed from years of planning mandatory weekly house changes, considered the costs. *Of course, Grace could do this*, she thought. *Her parents have plenty of money.*

"How would we pay the bills?" she asked.

"Well, I've thought about that," Grace said. "We could both get part-time jobs. All we have to pay for are gas and groceries. It'll be easy."

"I don't know, Grace," Ellie said. "That's a lot to take in."

"I don't know, Grace, that's a lot to take in," Grace mockingly repeated. "C'mon, Elles, we got this. Let's do it. Let's go on an adventure! Let's live *dangerously*."

Ellie stood quietly. That last word made her very uncomfortable.

Grace evaluated her friend's demeanor and said, "I'll tell you what. I need to make a list of things we'll need when we move in." Then, switching to an exaggerated accent, she said, "Why don't you stroll around the grounds, *dahling*, and take in Chez Grace?"

Ellie laughed. Grace reached for a pad of paper, and Ellie stepped out the back door and walked down toward the creek. Her mind was reeling. She was confused. Was this an opportunity of a lifetime she should take? It would give her freedom.

Or was this a dangerous move she would regret forever? She liked the idea of having one place to live. But there was something else inside her, arguing for the other side. Her mom wasn't the best, but she was still Mom, and she still provided some kind of protection.

Should she just look out for herself, or should she put her brother's needs ahead of hers? She pictured discussing it with her mother. She knew her mom didn't like her that much, but she couldn't imagine her allowing her to do something like this. Her dad probably would be glad to get rid of her. But you never know.

As she strolled along the creek, she saw an open field. Ellie sat down and looked at the water, while playing with the blade of grass in her hand, thinking. She lay back, the sunlight sharp in her eyes. Squinting, she raised a hand to shield her eyes and started talking out loud like she still often did with Mama Bunny.

She rehearsed the possible conversation with her mother. "Mom, I'm going to move in with Grace."

"Oh, Ellie," she said, mimicking her mother's voice. "You can't do that. I want you here."

Then, her mind pictured life without her mom and James. She would have to become even more grown-up than she already was. At least her mom kept the fridge stocked and the sheets clean. Moving to the cabin seemed like a risky decision.

"I don't think I'm ready to live like that yet," she said out loud, now rehearsing her next conversation. "I love you, Grace, but I don't think I can do this. There are bills and shopping and cleaning and ... oh, I wish someone would tell me what to do!" she finally exclaimed loudly.

Her private conversation was interrupted by another voice. "Tough decision?"

Ellie squinted. The voice sounded familiar, like her Grandma's, who had passed away five years earlier. The bright sun kept her from identifying who was talking to her.

"I know a little bit about that," the kind voice continued.

Ellie, startled, stood up and brushed the grass off her shirt. She saw an older woman standing next to her. The woman had silver-blonde hair, glasses with large, black rims, and was wearing blue jeans and a light sweater. Ellie also noticed she was wearing hiking boots.

Before she could say anything, the woman continued. "I'm sorry to intrude. I was going for a walk on this *beautiful* afternoon and heard you talking. I'm just a nosy old woman," she said with a laughing grunt. "And it sounded like maybe you could use someone to talk to. I can mind my own business if you want."

Ellie wasn't sure what to say or do. She wanted to be polite, but she didn't want to talk to a stranger.

"Well," the woman said, "I'll be on my way. It just helps me to talk things out sometimes. Have a *wonderful* afternoon," she said as she turned to walk away.

Maybe it was the woman's kind tone of voice or the fact that she reminded Ellie of the Grandma she dearly missed that gave Ellie pause. "Well," she said, loud enough for the woman to hear. The woman stopped and turned around, keeping her distance.

"It's just that my friend Grace wants me to move in with her up there," she said, pointing to the cabin in the distance. "And I don't think it's a good idea."

The older woman stood silently for a moment. She took a deep breath and said, "*That* cabin? No one has lived there for years. It sounds like it would be a hard thing to do."

Ellie watched as the hiking boots took a few steps toward her.

"When I was a young lady, about your age," the woman continued, "I faced something amazingly similar."

Ellie sat back down on the grass, followed by her newfound friend, who quietly groaned as she made herself comfortable on the ground next to Ellie.

"Tell me all about it," the woman said with a gentle, warm smile. Ellie started slowly, at first giving away very few details. But the more she talked, the more she found herself wanting to share. The woman seemed genuinely interested. She would nod at the right time, gasp occasionally when Ellie shared something gasp-worthy, and throw back her head with a genuine laugh when Ellie said something funny. Ellie found herself revealing more and more of her deeper feelings. It felt good to be listened to, understood, and supported. It was like Mama Bunny had started talking back to her.

Ellie finished the part about how her mom provided some stability in her life when they were interrupted by the sound of Grace's voice from the cabin, calling out to Ellie. "I guess I have to go," Ellie said.

"Yes, you must," the older woman said. "But before you do, can I share something? As I've listened to you share about this *difficult* situation, I have noticed something about you. You are a thoughtful, considerate, and strong person. You've got what it takes to make a good decision here. It's a long way from where you are to where I am. There are so many ups and downs, twists and turns … and I have a lot of confidence in your future."

"Thank you," Ellie said sincerely.

"I'm Elizabeth, by the way," the older woman said.

"That's cool," Ellie replied, "I'm Elizabeth too. I go by Ellie."

"Well, Ellie, it's nice to meet you. Have a great afternoon."

They both stood up and looked at each other.

Ellie smiled, turned, and started walking back to the cabin. She felt lighter and more confident. It was time to break the news to Grace. Ellie didn't turn around, but if she had, she would have only seen a wisp of vapor where Elizabeth had stood.

Ellie meets Elizabeth for the first time:
the Wise Woman within her made real.

From Elizabeth

Well, that was the first time Ellie and I officially met. Of course, I had always been there. But here, at the tender age of 17, Ellie finally reached out to me. She was looking for the path to her HeartPrint and needed guidance. I knew she would eventually say no to her dear friend's invitation. She just needed a little help in connecting with her truest self.

Your Wise Woman is always available as well. I hope you know what I'm talking about. She is the part of you that guides you to your HeartPrint. She is the internal voice of wisdom that all of us have. She usually comes to us in quiet moments, asking questions and making insightful observations. Do you talk to her? Does she answer?

Here, Ellie was conflicted. Her external life didn't match her internal wishes. Life just wasn't going the way she wanted. It was chaotic and jumbled, and Ellie felt misunderstood and not cared for by the adults in her life.

She needed a way to process those questions and conflicts. She needed context. She needed someone who could gently and warmly hold space for her. She needed someone who wasn't judgmental, so she could freely externalize her thoughts and feelings. *That* is what your Wise Woman does for you. She accepts us as we are without judgment. She values honesty. She helps you figure out your next best step. Yes, she sometimes speaks hard truths, but it's always with your best interest at heart.

And this isn't just Ellie's story. It reflects something happening around us as well. It seems to me that we've lost something in our world. Let's call it the intergenerational transfer of wisdom. It's been a part of our world for centuries. We yearn for it, but there is a general cultural malnourishment of *eldership* in our families and our communities. We are less as individuals because of its absence.

Let's face it. Confusion and pain are a part of the human experience. Have you ever felt like your world is unsettled and something just isn't right? Have you ever stuffed those feelings down and just moved on? It's understandable. This is what humans do as a way to cope. Unless we pull them out and resolve them, they just accumulate until they eventually spill over. Our Wise Woman helps us to resolve those feelings.

If we don't get them resolved, it's like carrying a cup of coffee up the stairs. If there's room in the cup, you can negotiate the trip without spilling anything. But when the cup is full, the coffee starts to slosh over the sides, spilling onto the stairs.

The coffee in the cup is like our pain and confusion. As long as they are a certain size, we can handle them. But as they accumulate and fill our cup, they eventually come to the point where they start spilling out into our relationships and daily experiences.

The "sloshing" might show up as being easily irritated. It can also make us distant and separated from those we love. That sloshing coffee can create a lot of chaos in our lives. Do you remember the open browser tabs? This is how they can affect us.

So, what can we do about the sloshing coffee? There is a decision that we have to make when we realize things aren't right. Simply put, we can either choose a Towards Move or an Away Move. One decision will move us toward our HeartPrint and the life we want to live. A different decision moves us away from it. The only way to make a Towards Move is by externalizing and processing our thoughts, questions, pain, and confusion until it is clear what action will allow us to take a step toward what is right for us.

Our default setting as humans under pressure is often to make an Away Move. It's the safest and easiest decision to make. It kicks the proverbial can down the road to be dealt with on another day.

Here's how it works. Our brain is wired, first and foremost, to *protect* us. If we don't bring our thoughts and feelings into our conscious mind and wrestle with them, our brain is left without any new information. It naturally takes us on the most direct path of protection.

That might mean yelling at someone. It might mean ignoring them. It may include a downward spiral of self-pity and withdrawal.

None of these will lead us toward our HeartPrint. But those actions *do solve* the immediate problem. Don't blame your beautiful brain. It's just doing what it's designed to do. It's the default setting.

I'm so grateful that I could help Ellie externalize her feelings and thoughts without judgment. Once she did, she could easily see the best way forward. That day, Ellie made a Towards Move, which meant choosing not to move in with Grace. I think Ellie's life would have been much more difficult if she had chosen differently.

I helped Ellie touch her HeartPrint that day. What she really wanted, deep down, was a couple of years more under her mom's protection, as imperfect as it was. She just wasn't ready to go it alone. Mom wasn't perfect. But she was, well, Mom.

I do want to mention that Ellie's friendship with Grace survived this incident. Grace decided not to move into the cabin either. They continued to draw closer and closer over the years.

There were many ups and downs over the next 11 years. Ellie would sometimes move toward her HeartPrint. But most of the time, she chose Away Moves. She just wasn't able yet to face all the questions her complicated life presented.

Ellie ended up going to pharmacy school, where, predictably, she got good grades. She was hired by a research firm and moved up quickly in the ranks because of her hard work and dedication. There were some boyfriends, but none of them seemed to work out. There was estrangement from her dad and a rocky relationship with her mom.

Over a decade after the cabin decision, things came to a head in an apartment in Waterbury, Connecticut. It was another terrifying moment for Ellie. She was living far from her HeartPrint and in survival mode. Also, a new character is introduced. Bridges is one of the greatest dogs ever. I can't wait for you to meet him.

A Cup of Tea with Meg

In this story, Ellie and Elizabeth meet for the first time. The connection to your Wise Woman is an essential part of your own journey and one that becomes clearer as you learn to listen and trust. For each of us, this is a special, precious, and deep connection. Here are some questions for you to ponder or discuss:

- Can you relate to the idea of having a Wise Woman? What does that mean to you?

- Can you describe your Wise Woman? Is she like Elizabeth? Do you communicate with her? How often do you get to feel her care and kindness?

- What about the sloshing coffee in your life? Can you identify something that keeps coming up in your life that affects your happiness and relationships?

Chapter 3 · Age 28

apartment 5C in Waterbury, Connecticut—a walk gone wrong

The fruit plate, usually impeccably arranged but today carelessly assembled, was quietly set on the glass kitchen table. Ellie looked out the window of her fourth-story apartment on another dreary winter day in Waterbury. Sighing, she sat down, alone, except for the ever-present Bridges, her Jack Russell terrier friend for the last year. The dog took its usual place next to her left leg under the table, patiently waiting for her to finish her breakfast and to hear the sound of the dishes clanking. That was the signal for his daily walk. Bridges, like most dogs, was acutely tuned in to Ellie's energy.

Ellie tried to eat, but only played with her breakfast. She sat silently without the background noise of the TV that was usually on. She lingered, contemplating her ever-growing sense of despair.

* * * *

She heard the voice of her *Inner Critic*.

You shouldn't feel this way. You are always finding a way to mess up your life. What is wrong with you?

* * * *

Ellie had a great job and had advanced to management in a short time. Yes, her relationship with her most recent boyfriend was strained, but that didn't account for the bad feelings that had become an ever-present part of her daily life.

She thought back to the few therapy sessions she had attended. They had helped a little, but were too far apart to do any real good. Her therapist was fine, but only fine. The sessions felt like a bandage placed on a gaping wound. It was expensive to get therapy, and the few times she'd started, she either couldn't afford to continue or had become frustrated trying to explain her family dynamics so the therapist could actually start helping her. She missed Grace. They hadn't talked in weeks, both being dragged in different directions due to careers and general life busyness. Ellie's spirits always lifted when she talked to Grace.

She dreaded going to work that day. She had made it this far by digging deep, overriding herself, and bringing a forced enthusiasm to her job. Ellie had lost her taste for life itself and, in quiet moments like this, she recognized the burgeoning feeling of emptiness and dissatisfaction.

※ ※ ※ ※

Blame-Shifting Self.

This is Cary's fault, she thought, picturing her boss being dismissive to her very real concerns about her work.

Her mind drifted back to a family party she had attended the month before where her mom had recounted the "that's not my baby" story. Her *Blame-Shifting Self* seethed with resentment.

What kind of mother tells a story like that? she thought. *It's her fault I feel so alone.*

Her *Blame-Shifting Self* kept going, this time focusing on her boyfriend.

Tommy is clueless, she thought. *He never asks how you're doing. He's so focused on himself, he can't even see you.*

Not even your own brother will listen to you, she concluded, completing the list of usual suspects. Her downward spiral list was complete, and then began again from the top. Each time she went through the list, she went deeper and deeper into rumination and helplessness, mixed with anger and contempt.

※ ※ ※ ※

Ellie was alone and desperate.

She was interrupted by Bridges. He usually showed excitement about his morning walk, but today, he gently nuzzled Ellie's leg with his nose, sensing her frame of mind.

"Okay, little guy, let's go," she said out loud, eliciting a tiny, excited bark from Bridges. She left the dishes on the table, slipped on her coat, and put the leash on her dog. As they headed toward the elevator, Ellie looked at Bridges's enthusiasm. *Wow. I can't remember being that excited about anything,* she thought.

Ellie felt the brisk winter wind hit her face as they left the building. Her steps started to feel heavier and heavier as they clomped down the sidewalk. Her mind was distracted, and her stomach was churning. She didn't pay attention as Bridges tugged on his leash.

After walking a couple of blocks, Ellie and Bridges stopped at the red light on the corner. When the light turned green, she absentmindedly stepped into the street, ready to cross the road. Just then, she heard a loud honk as a garbage truck rolled by her, barely missing her. The driver angrily blasted their horn again and yelled at her to watch what she was doing. She jumped back onto the sidewalk, narrowly avoiding being struck.

Ellie stood there, wide-eyed and frozen. She felt her heart racing. Bridges first tugged on the leash, but then, a few seconds later, sat down next to her, looking up at her expectantly.

"I can't do this," she said to herself, trembling from head to toe. "I just can't. I can't live like this anymore."

Her mind was drained. Her spirit was depleted. She felt it in her arms, legs, and feet. But she felt it mostly in her chest. It was debilitating. It felt like an ending, like there was nothing else she could do. It was over.

Ellie was a relentless person, and her determination had served her well up to now. She had learned to push down her emotions and push forward with life. But finally, there were no more places left to push things.

Here, at the stoplight, with Bridges in tow, she reached her limit. She couldn't even bring herself to get her flip phone from her coat pocket and call in sick. She stood there with Bridges patiently sitting at her side. Eventually, she pulled her phone from her pocket and called work. Then she slowly walked back to her building, went up in the elevator, unlocked the door to her apartment, let Bridges off the leash, and sat on the couch with her coat still on.

Ellie's eyes grew heavy, and she drifted into a deep, uncomfortable, and dreamless sleep. The doorbell rang, startling her. She opened her eyes and took a deep breath. She walked across the kitchen and opened the door.

"Hello, Ellie," the woman standing at the door said with a gentle smile. Ellie remembered the face and the voice from years earlier. It was Elizabeth. She had the same silver-blonde hair and black-rimmed glasses as before. Ellie looked down and noticed she also had the same hiking boots. This time, though, she was wearing a big, furry overcoat.

Before Ellie could say anything, Elizabeth continued. "Can I come in?" she asked. Caught off guard, Ellie stepped back and opened the door the rest of the way.

"Yes, please come in," Ellie said politely but quietly, still numb from the near-miss.

"You still have your coat on. Are you cold?" Elizabeth asked as she removed her own coat and threw it over the back of the nearby couch. Ellie noticed Elizabeth was wearing the same jeans as when they'd met.

"Yes, I guess I am," Ellie replied. Ellie was confused. Was she cold or warm? She was disoriented and depleted, and her body felt unfamiliar, like it wasn't hers at all.

"It's so cold outside!" Elizabeth said, rubbing her hands together. "I could sure use something to warm me up."

"Uh, I have tea," Ellie said.

"Marvelous!" Elizabeth said. "What a beautiful apartment you have!" she added enthusiastically as she walked around surveying the room. "It matches your personality. It's so *orderly* and neat. I like it."

Again, before Ellie could respond, Elizabeth continued.

"And this must be your faithful companion," she said, glancing at Bridges, who was sleeping on a nearby chair.

Ellie was surprised that Bridges didn't even wake up. He would usually go crazy at the slightest noise.

"Yes, that's Bridges," Ellie said as she put the pot on the stove.

"Bridges? That's an unusual name for a dog."

Ellie smiled. "Yes, he's named after Jeff Bridges, the actor."

"Oh," Elizabeth replied with a big smile. "Quite clever. I see the resemblance."

Ellie looked up, and Elizabeth was sitting on the couch. "Come here, Ellie," she said, patting the cushion next to her. "Let's talk."

Ellie brought the tea, set it on the table, and sat down. Ellie was glad to at least have someone else in the room with her.

"First things first," Elizabeth began. "I know it's been a while. Are you happy about the decision you made about the cabin?"

Ellie couldn't recall what Elizabeth was talking about. Her mind was confused. "I don't know," was all she could muster.

"That's okay. Tell me about this morning," Elizabeth said, looking into Ellie's eyes.

Ellie averted her gaze but felt the urge to share openly.

"I don't understand it," she started, staring straight ahead. "I just couldn't make my body move anymore. I used to be able to push through times like this. It's something I've done my whole life. Today, something just got in my way. Something stopped me, and I don't know what it was."

"Hmm," Elizabeth replied. "That's really hard. What did it feel like?"

"Well," Ellie continued, "My breath was in my throat. My chest felt so ... heavy. I couldn't move. I tried. But I just couldn't do it."

"That's so scary," the woman said. "It's like you couldn't get enough air? Was it hard to breathe?"

Ellie sighed deeply. "Yes, exactly. I couldn't catch my breath." She felt her shoulders relax slightly, and she turned toward Elizabeth.

"Have you ever felt this way before?" Elizabeth asked quietly.

Ellie stared straight ahead again. "It reminds me of when I was a kid and got thrown off my bike. I couldn't breathe. But nothing like today. I've always just pushed through. This time, I couldn't. It was too much."

They sat silently for a few minutes while Elizabeth sipped her tea. Ellie sat motionless, shoulders hunched, head down, and hands clenched.

"Well," Elizabeth said, "I'm proud of you."

Ellie looked at her. "Proud of me?"

"Yes," she replied. "You know something now you didn't know this morning. You know that pushing through doesn't work anymore. That's pretty big stuff."

"I'm not feeling very proud of myself," Ellie said, looking at the floor.

Elizabeth chuckled. "Well, I'll be the judge of that," she said. "There is definitely work to be done," she continued. "Let me ask you this: What do you think is the most important thing to do *right now*?"

Ellie thought for a moment.

Chapter 3 • Age 28

"Tell me what your body feels like," Elizabeth prompted her. "Start with your shoulders."

"Well, they hurt. And I've got a headache. And look at my hands!" Ellie held out her clenched fists.

"I'm so sorry," Elizabeth said. "Okay. Let's start with a deep breath together," she said as she inhaled a full, deep breath.

Ellie followed her lead.

"Now," Elizabeth continued, "Let's work on those shoulders. Relax them."

Ellie tried to relax her shoulders. She began to feel some relief.

"Next, let those beautiful fingers of yours uncurl."

Ellie followed the instructions, slowly loosening her fingers.

"Let's try another deep breath," Elizabeth continued.

They repeated the sequence a few times, and each time Ellie felt her body relax more. She felt calmer, more in control.

"Now, close your eyes," Elizabeth finally said. "Your journey continues …"

Ellie closed her eyes. When she opened them, it was only herself and Bridges. She looked around the room; Elizabeth was nowhere to be seen. Next, she looked at her unclenched hands. She realized that her headache was gone. She was breathing normally. She closed her eyes again, hoping Elizabeth would reappear, but to no avail. "I miss her already," she said to Bridges.

Ellie freezes as the truck roars past,
with Bridges waiting patiently at her side.

From Elizabeth

This was an important moment. Ellie had pushed down her questions, pain, and confusion for so long that she had reached her limit. It was like there were finally too many browser tabs open and too much coffee in the sloshing cup. Something had to change.

Before she could start moving toward her HeartPrint, she first needed to deal with the immediate situation. Ellie had to learn how to get past this difficult moment.

There were many things I knew Ellie would need to eventually face, but here she had more pressing issues. She had to be able to return to her body and have the distress leave it. So, I worked with her to regulate her body. That's the thing about us Wise Women. We never ask you to do something you can't do. Sometimes, just getting through a moment is the best thing possible.

Moments like hers are not uncommon, and you may have felt something similar yourself. You see, there are two parts to our nervous system: the sympathetic nervous system and the parasympathetic nervous system. They operate very differently. Our sympathetic nervous system engages when we face danger. Our parasympathetic nervous system can only engage when we feel safe.

In times of high stress, when we are flooded with emotion like Ellie was on the corner, our sympathetic nervous system engages in order to protect us. If we don't reset ourselves, we go on to the next stage. You may have heard of it. It's called *fight or flight*, and we can add *freeze* to that. When this happens, our beautiful brain takes over our bodies. It is on high alert, and we enter survival mode. It is exhausting, physically depleting, and can be debilitating.

When we reach this state, a lot of things happen to us. Remember, job one for our brain is to protect us. Everything in our body is directed by our brain to focus on the immediate dangerous situation and *get safe*. Our palms sweat, our hands clench, and our breathing gets shallow. If something is non-essential, it gets shut out. Stress hormones get secreted. Glucose is released to help us think faster.

We get tunnel vision and see only the things needed for survival at that moment. It affects our sight, hearing, touch, and even smell.

That's exactly where Ellie was when she was standing on that corner. She had reached her limit. It wasn't just the physical danger from the near-miss with the garbage truck. It was the underlying accumulation of what was happening in her life at the time and, most of all, her unhelpful, circular, ruminative thoughts.

As humans, we have the blessing and the curse of busy brains. For instance, if we relive a dangerous situation in our mind, we will have very similar physiological responses as though we were actually in that moment in the very same situation we are imagining. It's as if we are going through it in real life. If we aren't able to resolve the stress we feel while reliving it, our body will go into the fight-or-flight response.

Ellie had spent the morning rehashing her negative situation. That was the foundation for what happened next. Already in a heightened state when the garbage truck nearly hit her, she was taken over the edge. And this time, she didn't have the resources to come back.

Although Ellie was very successful in her job, it didn't mean she was immune to this cycle. This is something that is hardwired into our DNA as the result of centuries of evolution. Have you ever just pushed down your emotions and moved forward? When we keep doing this over and over, it overrides our true selves. It might work for a while, but there comes a time of reckoning when something fundamental must be addressed.

Before Ellie could do any serious work and move toward her HeartPrint, she had to solve the immediate problem—her body was overloaded. Only then could she have the energy to approach the underlying issues. She was not attuned to her HeartPrint, which caused stress and made it increasingly difficult for her to handle her unanswered questions. Then, when a dangerous situation arose, she froze.

You may have been there before. What causes you to get into this fight, flight, or freeze state? Perhaps it's when you get into a heated argument and you feel yourself shutting down. Maybe your children's behavior overwhelms your system. Or, like Ellie, it could be things like stress at work. When you find yourself feeling like this, the first thing to do is deal with the immediate situation.

It's important to first take the time to *get out* of the situation and reset your body. You are of no use to yourself or anyone else when your nervous system is overwhelmed. After regulating it, you can approach the problems in front of you with a new perspective.

To alleviate this heightened state, it helps to *externalize* your feelings. As long as they stay inside you, they will control you. Externalizing means your feelings and thoughts come out of your mind and go *somewhere*. You could simply speak them out loud. Or, if it's easier for you, write them down. As simple as this sounds, I know it's hard.

Ellie needed to talk about her shoulders, her chest, and her hands. Only then could she start the process of regulation. Once her thoughts were externalized, she was able to take some deep breaths and get through the crisis she was facing. I knew that she saw herself as a strong and "grind-it-out" gal. I knew it was hard for her to admit how weak and helpless she felt. She thought that she *shouldn't* feel a certain way, so she decided she didn't feel that way. Maybe you can relate.

We unleash the power of our HeartPrint when we start to honestly express our feelings and thoughts. And your Wise Woman holds space for those feelings and thoughts without judgment. This was an important step forward for our dear Ellie. It would take some time, but she learned a valuable lesson that cold winter afternoon.

Okay, enough about all that. Our next story happens a few years later. It's when Ellie decided a guy called Joe was someone she should hold on to. Our lives aren't perfect. However, I'm glad that for Ellie, there were some perfect moments along the way. Even when we are struggling to connect with our HeartPrint, we can experience the good stuff that life can bring. Joe was the very definition of *the good stuff*. I'm looking forward to you getting to know him. But first, Meg.

A Cup of Tea with Meg

Here, Ellie is in crisis. Things had built up in her until she finally froze. She needed a way to get through the moment, and Elizabeth helped her with that. Take some time to consider these questions:

- Have you ever experienced a moment like the one Ellie did? What happened? What was it like? What did you learn or decide from that experience? Something that allowed you to heal and grow and move toward your HeartPrint? Or something that didn't help you heal and moved you away from your HeartPrint?

- Can you identify any ongoing, underlying stress in your life that creates an environment for you to experience the fight, flight, or freeze states of mind?

- Could you make any decisions today that would support your body and mind to find access to peace?

Chapter 4 · Age 31

a light-blue Honda on a drive back from the Poconos—the future looks bright

The fully packed car finished the descent from the mountains of Pennsylvania, pulled onto Interstate 84, and headed east. Inside, there was Ellie, her dog Bridges, and Joe, her boyfriend of nine months. The bright morning sun caused both of them to lower their sun visors. They were returning from Joe's family reunion at Birchwood Lakes in the Poconos.

It was the first time that Ellie had met any of Joe's extended family. Unlike Ellie, who just had James, Joe had two brothers and two sisters. They had all been there, along with Joe's parents, some aunts and uncles, and six younger nieces and nephews. It was their custom to gather together every couple of years to spend a few days, eat homemade meals, the preparation of which was assigned to the different families, play games, and catch up on one another's lives. It seemed very normal to Joe. But not to Ellie.

Joe had been quiet for the first 20 minutes of the trip back, as he focused on the winding road getting them to the freeway. The song "Firework" by Katy Perry was playing softly in the background. When it ended, Ellie turned off the radio.

"Your sister Charlotte and I got to know each other pretty well," she said, petting Bridges.

"Oh yeah?" Joe answered, "Great!"

"She told me something about you," Ellie continued.

"What was that?" Joe asked with a slight smile.

"She said that you've *always* been the quiet one."

"Well," Joe replied, "I guess that's true." Then, after a moment of silence, he added, "That's not a claim that Charlotte could ever make."

They both chuckled. "Yes," Ellie said, "she is a talker." After a moment, Ellie asked, "Did you enjoy the visit? You seemed to keep to yourself a lot."

"Oh, I had a great time," Joe said. "We all sort of fall into our roles when we get together. It's always been like that. Charlotte talks, Dave tells stories, and Sara always has her drama."

"And what's your role?" Ellie asked.

Joe laughed. "I guess I'm the audience. It's okay. I like it."

Joe fell silent again. Ellie absentmindedly petted Bridges. She thought back on the last few days. There had been laughter, good-natured teasing, and a kind of rhythm to the family's relationships that Ellie was deeply attracted to. She smiled as she remembered helping with the dishes as Dave told a story about a snake on a fishing trip.

It all felt completely new to her, yet somehow familiar in a way her HeartPrint had always known. Everyone seemed to accept her without even knowing her. She didn't have anything to prove to them. There were no strings attached. It was a kind of love that asked nothing in return. She didn't know she had missed it until she experienced it.

"Well, I liked it," she said quietly. "Being around all of them."

Joe smiled, not taking his eyes off the road. "I'm glad. We should do it together again next time."

Ellie smiled again at the thought of returning with Joe.

"Have you ever wished you had a big family?" Joe asked.

"I guess so. A long time ago. But it didn't seem like it was in the cards," Ellie replied.

"Maybe the deck is changing," Joe said, glancing at Ellie.

Ellie reached over and touched Joe on the knee. "I think I would like that," she said.

Just then, Bridges sneezed loudly, interrupting the moment. Then he sneezed twice more, like he was making a point. Joe and Ellie laughed out loud. The sun dipped behind a cloud and Ellie turned the radio back on.

She leaned back and started humming "Sweet Home Alabama" along with the radio. She wasn't sure how this relationship would turn out, but for now, she felt as though she was exactly where she should be.

She wasn't sure how this whole relationship would turn out, but for now, she felt like she was exactly where she should be.

From Elizabeth

It's a funny thing. Our lives are not made up of all good things or all bad things. We have our struggles, and we also have our precious moments. Yes, there may be issues we have to handle within ourselves, but we can still have days, weeks, and months when things are pretty great.

This was a happy season for Ellie. Being around Joe's family made a connection she hadn't had before. There's something special about being in a group where we are loved and accepted, along with our quirks and weaknesses. Ellie didn't feel that very much growing up, but she felt it here. She craved the normalcy of that kind of life, and Joe gave it to her.

I wasn't needed so much during this time. I like that. Real life is full of surprising moments that give us wisdom if we are open to it. There was a time when Ellie would have withdrawn because she felt out of place. But it was a meaningful moment when she decided to lean into the love that was offered to her. That is the wisdom she found. She accepted what was in front of her, even though she didn't think she deserved it yet.

Yes, underlying it all were all of the unanswered questions she had. She wondered if she would repeat her mother's mistakes. She felt insecure about her ability to have a lifelong relationship. There was a lot more she would have to organize into her filing cabinets and build on. But for now, the joy she felt was hers to keep.

Well, in case you haven't figured it out, Joe and Ellie got married shortly after that trip. They had their ups and downs (mostly ups), but when Ellie became pregnant with Chase, challenges arose. Ellie changed. Joe didn't know how to handle it. It led to a tough time in a hotel room. I was needed once again.

A Cup of Tea with Meg

I love this story! Here are some great questions for your consideration about what was discussed in this chapter:

- What's a perfect day from your memories?
- What made it so wonderful?
- How might you honor that experience and remember the goodness of it more?
- Could you add anything into your current life that would awaken this experience or create an equivalent one for you?

Chapter 5 · Age 33

the Coonamessett Hotel outside of Falmouth, Massachusetts—alone and desperate

"You aren't due for two weeks!"

Joe and Ellie were in a hotel, and it was *tense*.

"I *have* to go on this trip," Joe insisted. "With you on maternity leave, we can't afford for me to lose my job." Joe changed his tone. "It will be fine," he said more gently. "I'll call you every day. My cab is here. I have to go to the airport."

Ellie stared out the window at a beautiful park across the street. "Fine," was all she could manage. "I'll see you back home."

Joe picked up his suitcase and headed toward the door. "I'll call you tonight," he said as he left.

Ellie went over and lay down on the bed. She wrapped her arms around her stomach, unconsciously protecting her unborn child. She lay there until long after the sun had set, but couldn't fall asleep.

* * * *

Her *Anxious Self* took over.

It wasn't so much the thoughts she had, although they were tricky. It was a gnawing, churning feeling in her stomach. It was more images and scenes playing out in her mind. She pictured herself alone with a crying baby. She imagined night after night of no sleep and being exhausted. She visualized herself breastfeeding, failing, and not knowing how to take care of her baby. She grew even more anxious.

She wanted so much to be a good mother, but dreaded the thought she would fail. She fretted about Joe and what would happen if he left, like her dad had.

※ ※ ※ ※

So, what was supposed to be a final getaway before the baby was born turned out to be a string of escalating arguments, mostly started by Ellie. She was stressed and felt unsupported by her husband, and unloved and unsupported by her mom (again).

She had hoped her parents might change when she got pregnant. But her dad had shown little interest in his soon-to-be grandson. Her mother seemed to try, but, as always, had something more important to do. She often silently cursed them. Even Grace was absent, busy with her wedding plans.

Ellie began to cry. "I can't let this child live like this," she said aloud. Grasping her tummy tighter, she spoke to her unborn baby: "I can't pass this life on to you."

She feared that her own loneliness might one day become her child's, and that thought was crushing. Each day she felt a little more fragile, a little more exposed. She tried to soothe herself in the way she always had. She turned to Joe, hoping he could share the weight. But he wasn't able to help in these moments, so the feelings didn't ease. Instead, Ellie found herself stockpiling memories of times she'd asked for comfort and hadn't felt supported, each one confirming her sense of being alone in this.

Ellie had made some strides in her growth over the past few years. She was seeing a therapist and thought she might be growing into someone who was healing. But the pregnancy had changed things. Her emotions were different. Her vulnerability was bringing the pain and confusion below the surface uncomfortably close.

She was understandably using every bit of her daily energy just to cope. Instead of drawing energy from her Wise Woman, she was burning through what little she had just to stay afloat. Her focus narrowed to her ever-changing body, and everything else drifted out of reach. She didn't have the time or capacity she once did. Old, painful patterns were returning.

Her *Anxious Self* ruminated on what kind of dad Joe would be. She questioned the very decision to bear a child. She didn't know how her career was supposed to work. There were so many unanswered questions. Her body had been transformed into something that sometimes felt ugly. She was constantly tired, achy, and grumpy. No matter what she did, she couldn't seem to escape.

Finally, Ellie fell into a light slumber. She dreamed of herself and Grace traveling together on a train. She kept looking for her friend but could never seem to find her. It disturbed her enough that she twisted on the bed. This small movement woke her.

When she opened her eyes, Elizabeth was sitting on the bed next to her, quietly crying.

"You've been through so much," Elizabeth whispered. "It's okay. I'm here."

"Oh, Elizabeth," Ellie murmured. "I'm so glad you're here. I don't know what to do."

Quietly, Elizabeth let her tears fall down her cheeks.

"It hurts so much," Ellie said, and began to sob.

"I know," Elizabeth said. "I know. Let it out. I'm here, I will always be here."

After a few minutes, Elizabeth said calmly, "So, tell me."

Ellie began to talk to her now trustworthy friend. She shared about her dad, her mom, Joe, and Grace. She shared about how alone she felt. She ended with, "I'm afraid that this one will have a lonely life, too," as she patted her stomach.

"I know it doesn't feel this way right now, but you've got this," Elizabeth said firmly. "The fact that you care so much about your child tells me everything I need to know. You've learned a lot about loneliness. Of course, this child will sometimes feel lonely. But there's a difference. They will have someone to talk to. It might be hard to understand now," Elizabeth continued, "but this pain is also your teacher. I want to invite you to honor it and embrace it. It can lead you in the right direction if you let it."

After another moment of silence, Elizabeth said, "You have to find a way back to your HeartPrint. For now, close your eyes and get some sleep. You need your energy." She took Ellie's hand and said, "I'll stay right here with you."

Ellie didn't understand what her HeartPrint was, but she was too tired to ask. She obediently closed her eyes and, for the first time in weeks, fell into a deep and restful sleep. She was awakened by a phone call four hours later. Her arm was still lying in a position as though she was holding someone's hand.

It was Joe on the phone, letting her know he'd arrived safely.

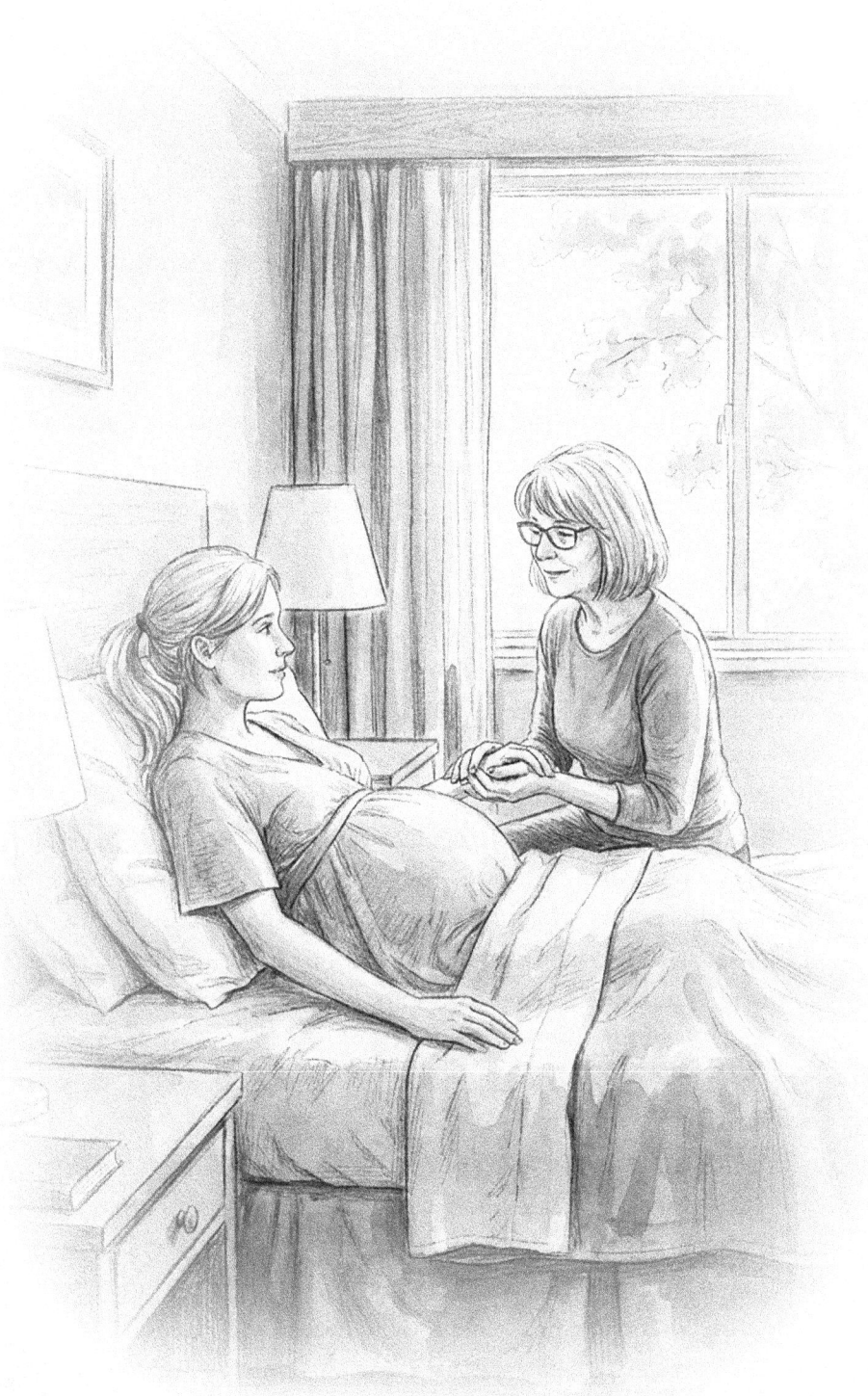

"You've been through so much," Elizabeth whispered.
"It's okay. I'm here."

From Elizabeth

Well, that was quite a story. It was a sad moment. And it was the beginning of some deep healing. I could be there for her in a way that Ellie had craved from her own parents and husband. It's often just how life is. She had her tough times, like she did in the hotel room, where deep healing was needed. And she had her great times, like the family reunions with Joe, and great, fun weekends at the cabin with Grace that healed her in a different way. Ellie even had good memories of her mom and dad. It might feel like I am sharing more of the hard stories than the good ones, but rest assured, every pain and heartache is information and fuel leading Ellie closer to her most congruent HeartPrint self. Just stay tuned.

Here, Ellie was coming face-to-face with some of the foundational issues that affected her sense of safety and belonging in the world. She felt alone. She really wanted to live a good and fulfilling life, but she had an aching loneliness that only her grandmother understood, and she just didn't have the tools to work through all of those browser tabs and sloshing coffee cups. At different times along her life, she was more connected to her HeartPrint, but, as it turned out, living the truest version of herself often proved elusive.

This is a universal human experience. There is no escaping heartache and pain. It may or may not be loneliness for you. However, we all have something foundational that belongs to us and us alone, which must be worked through. If we can identify it, we can grow through it.

Ellie did undergo some healing on this day, but at the same time, her focus was on her baby. She wouldn't get serious and really deal with these deeper issues for another eight years. Maybe it's because life happens so fast when we are younger. There are things like school, jobs, dating, marriage, pregnancy, and children. As wonderful as all of those things are, they sometimes can distract us from pursuing our HeartPrint.

Sometimes we are going along just fine, and then something happens. We have moments, like this one in the hotel room, where we just can't ignore the fundamental questions about life. It's only when we have reached some kind of tipping point, often later in life, that we are compelled to begin this process. It's usually linked to a major life event that pulls the rug out from under our feet, like the birth of a child, the death of a Loved One, a job loss, infidelity, divorce, or an ending we find heartbreaking. In times like these, as I told Ellie, it's essential to acknowledge and embrace the pain, rather than ignore it.

I have found that the pain and confusion we feel in life can point us in the right direction, if we let it. It shows us the next thing for us to work on. Each time we follow the pain, it leads us closer to our HeartPrint. I guess what I am saying is that our pain, confusion, and questions are not the enemies. They can be our teachers, if we let them.

You may have noticed that we have met some interesting parts of Ellie. We've seen her *Inner Critic*, her *Blame-Shifting Self*, and her *Anxious Self*. There are more.

Interestingly, each of these parts wants to serve us in some way. They aim to protect us, and they allow us to cope with difficult and stressful situations. And as much as they want to come to our defense, they can't be allowed to run the show. If they are the ones defining our trajectory, we will end up in a downward spiral, further and further from our HeartPrint. It feels good in the moment when these parts of us are in charge, but it's an illusion.

I call these different parts of us the *Shadow Sisters*. Each of us has them. They are the parts of us that have learned how to deal with threats. They come to our rescue to get us to safety as quickly as possible. They want to protect us. Many of the *Shadow Sisters* come from our childhood. They develop as ways to cope with and adapt to life. They become a part of who we are.

Instead of hating them or trying to throw them out of our lives, I invite you to listen to them. They are only trying to help. The trick is to learn to listen to the essence of what some part of yourself is trying to communicate to you, without letting this inflamed part have ultimate control of your life. That position of leadership is reserved for your Wise Woman, not your hurt selves. Understanding and caring for these different parts of ourselves, closing one browser tab at a time, is a big part of being able to live more and more from our HeartPrint.

Let's go back to the hotel room. A few weeks later, Ellie's incredible son Chase was born. He was always one of the singular joys of her life. Ellie and Chase had their ups and downs, as you will see later, but he turned out to be a great man. I am so glad Ellie learned her life lessons along the way and passed those on to Chase. It wasn't just Chase whose life was transformed by Ellie's growth. Chase's daughter benefited as well. And I like to think about *her* children and grandchildren. I guess what I'm saying is that any transformation we go through doesn't just make our lives better; it changes future generations (and very often influences our family of origin as well).

Our next story happens another eight years later. Ellie eventually returned to work and moved on with her life. She had some good times and bad times. She still wasn't ready to dive deep into the issues. So, as you can probably guess, she continued to face different crises that came and went. They were solved in the moment, but her underlying pain and confusion were never addressed. So, there were more and more browser tabs opened and more coffee spilled.

I'm amazed at how we, as humans, are able to compartmentalize and avoid our pain. I wonder why. Maybe it's because we don't have the skills to do something different, so we just push them down. It wasn't until she was in her 40s that Ellie was ready to do the deep work needed to heal the pain and confusion blocking her connection to her Wise Woman self, and thereby locate and live more deeply from her HeartPrint.

A Cup of Tea with Meg

This story is about learning from our pain and recognizing our *Shadow Sisters*. I hope these questions will help you sift and sort through your own *Shadow Sisters*:

- What painful experiences like Ellie's have you had? Make a list for yourself.
- Reflecting on these pain points, see if you can take a 10,000-foot view and look down on them. Can you see how they helped you grow from that experience into a stronger and wiser version of yourself? Can you see any jewels and gifts amid the pain?
- Can you make a preliminary list of your *Shadow Sisters*? Which ones show up the most in your life? What pain points are they trying to defend and protect?

Chapter 6 · Age 41

the messy back porch outside of New Haven, Connecticut—distraught and disconnected

After a long, mostly productive day at work, Ellie pressed the remote control and slowly pulled into her parking spot in the garage. Turning off the car, she breathed a sigh of relief. "*That* was a long day," she said to herself. She gathered her laptop bag, purse, and water bottle and headed toward the door to the house.

Along the way, the metal water bottle slipped out of her hands, making a loud crashing sound as it hit the floor. The sound made Ellie jump backward, knocking her shoulder hard against the door frame. Rubbing her shoulder, she felt a hot flash of irritation at her clumsiness. She picked up the water bottle and wedged it securely into her laptop bag. Instead of making two trips, she loaded herself up and continued the short walk to the kitchen door. She bent over awkwardly and twisted the door handle. She pushed the door open with her sore shoulder, wincing slightly, expecting the smell of dinner being prepared, but there was nothing.

She placed the items on the counter, hung up her jacket, and, as she washed her hands, surveyed her home. In the dining room sat Chase, now eight years old, playing a video game with his headphones on. Glancing over, she made a note of the sink full of unwashed dishes. She let out a small, frustrated grunt. Her resentment was building fast. She walked into the family room where her husband, Joe, was watching TV.

"Hey," she said flatly to him.

"Hey!" Joe said without taking his eyes off the TV. "You won't believe this. The Celtics are killing the Lakers."

Ellie stood there.

Her *Angry Self* was putting the final touches to a well-rehearsed speech. Before she could start, she was interrupted by their new puppy, Hunter, barking.

"No one has fed you?" she asked loud enough for Joe to hear. Her *Angry Self* made sure that the tone of her voice communicated her irritation, but Joe didn't seem to notice. She walked back to the kitchen, where she saw the brown pile that let her know Hunter had also not been let out.

※ ※ ※ ※

Her *Angry Self* was now sitting at the head of the table.

He is such a jerk, she thought contemptuously. *He cares more about a basketball game than his family. Look at Chase sitting with that game when he could be doing something with his dad. He doesn't touch the dishes, he doesn't feed the dog, and he doesn't even let him out to poop! What is wrong with him?*

※ ※ ※ ※

Ellie's blood pressure was already high as she transitioned from a long day into her home, where nothing was the way she wanted it to be. Now, her frustration was building to a breaking point.

She cleaned up the mess, making as much noise as she could. Hunter, sensing the tension in the room, continued to bark louder and louder.

"Alright, alright," she said angrily, "Hold on to your horses."

"Hunter!" Joe shouted. "Ellie, please. I'm watching the game here."

Ellie stood in the kitchen, not sure what to do. She was at full tilt. She quickly fed Hunter, glanced into the dining room, and saw that Chase, lost in his video game, hadn't noticed anything. She started muttering sarcastically under her breath. "No problems here, sweetheart. I've just been at work all day. Let me feed the dog, clean up his mess, and do the dishes. Oh, *and* make dinner. I love being the only adult in the house. It's what I live for."

She opened the door to let Hunter out and followed him onto the patio. Although it was one of her favorite places, all she could notice was the work that needed to be done. There were two empty beer cans sitting on the table. The wooden patio was covered with dust. The ferns were wilting, and she hadn't even put out her autumn decorations. *I just can't keep up with all of this,* she thought.

Ellie took a deep breath of fresh air. That helped some. So, she did it again. Then she started to move her body, stretching a little this way and that, helping a little more.

Then she noticed the sun setting, and dusk gathering. That helped even more.

She walked over, picked up one of the beer cans, and then set it down again.

Ellie sighed deeply, feeling the flare of anger rise again. She breathed again, trying to let the anger go. She reminded herself that this was her favorite time of the day. She closed her eyes and drew another intentional breath.

When she opened them, she was startled by the presence of someone else near the patio. They were standing in the shadows under her beautiful Japanese maple. Ellie idly noticed that it had weeds around the base of it. It had been years since she had seen Elizabeth. "Tough day?" Elizabeth asked, emerging from the shadows.

It was comforting to see her old friend. Ellie calmed down a little more.

"It's been a while," Elizabeth continued softly. "Tell me what's going on."

Without hesitation, Ellie began to describe her day. She had gone through a successful but stressful day at work, where she had completed a project to the praise of her boss. She had got stuck in traffic on the way home. She went through the details of her disastrous entry home and shared about the dishes, the dog, the lack of dinner, and her family's obliviousness.

Elizabeth listened attentively. Ellie told her that she wanted to go into the living room and let Joe have what he deserved. She shared about how she felt unappreciated and unloved. She finished by saying, "Everyone in this home is disconnected and in their own world. I'm the only one trying to pull it together. Joe just doesn't care."

Ellie sighed as she finished her story.

"Yes," Elizabeth said, "that *was* a tough day." She smiled. "I can't believe how much Chase has grown up!" she said, changing the subject. "And look at how far you've come. You're doing a fantastic job as a wife and a mother."

Ellie noticed Elizabeth was wearing a dusky blue cashmere wrap to keep warm and the same black-rimmed glasses as before. She wore a large, silver, leaf-shaped pendant that caught the fading light of the evening. Ellie was struck by her quiet elegance.

Elizabeth let out a deep sigh. "So, let's start with what you wish had happened. That will help us understand what's needed right now. Then, we can think about how to proceed."

Ellie thought for a minute.

"Well, I wish things had been under control when I came home," she began. "I think I need to calm down for a minute. And, I don't think I will go in there and blow things up. I've done that before and I've always regretted it."

"Great decision," Elizabeth said with a wry smile.

Ellie continued. "I guess I just have to get through the next couple of hours. I'll get a pizza from the freezer and preheat the oven. I'll let Chase know we will eat in 20 minutes. I'll see if the game is over, and if it is, I'll ask Joe to get started on the dishes. Then I'll go upstairs, change into my PJs, and wash my face."

"Perfect," Elizabeth said optimistically. "And …?"

"And when the night is over, I'll sit down and figure out how to make this better going forward. I know Joe is not my enemy. It just feels that way now."

Elizabeth stepped back and looked at Ellie. "You certainly have come a long way," she said. "It's beautiful to see you open up to the wisdom that's always been yours."

Elizabeth turned and walked toward the woods, her silhouette fading into the dusk. Ellie lingered a moment, then moved to open the door. Hunter was there waiting, tail wagging gently.

She stepped back into the kitchen, opened the freezer, flicked on the oven, and began the process of building something better for herself and for her family.

It was comforting to see her old friend. Ellie calmed down a little more.

From Elizabeth

I was always only a quiet moment away from Ellie. Sometimes, we just need someone to talk to. And sometimes, the best person for us is our Wise Woman, who reminds us of what *really* matters to us and helps us sift and sort through the next right steps that lift us out of the hard times and into something that better serves us. This was a tough day underpinned by hunger, fatigue, and responsibility, but it was a typical day for this stage in Ellie's life.

Ellie was in that familiar state we all recognize: stressed out. This is a common condition in our modern age. For sure, stress has always been a part of the human experience. However, before the advent of technology, industries that required us to have specific jobs, the need to earn an income, our reliance on transportation, and our thousand-mile-an-hour lifestyles, stress would arise, be faced, be resolved, and then disappear. When a lion or tiger confronted our ancestors in the savannah, they would certainly experience stress. But when the threat ended, so did their stress.

That's not how it works for us. We face stressful situations daily, and the stress accumulates. It's because we are constantly facing perceived danger after perceived danger. It's not a literal life-and-death experience we are facing, like a lion stalking us on the savannah. Instead, it's the relentless psychological stress of trying to dot every *i* and cross every *t*. Our bodies treat these perceived threats as real.

These situations open tabs in our browser, overwhelming and then depleting our system. Over time, the stress accumulates to levels we call burnout. Or, they become illnesses and breakdowns. All of this adds to our pain and confusion. We ask ourselves questions like, *Why can't I be successful?* and *Why do other people seem to be able to cope with this life when I can't?* We start to question ourselves, which contributes even more to our stress.

We also face different *kinds* of stress than our ancestors faced. For us, it's usually emotional threats, not physical ones. We face things like the cost of living and our children's safety, especially when we aren't with them. There are just too many things to do in too short a time. It's unrelenting. The lion, as it were, is constantly nipping at our heels.

Think about how stressful our lives are. We have pressure to perform at work. There is pressure at home and in our relationships. Just driving down the highway can be a stressful event. Add to that our aspirations and desire to experiment with new things, and we become, like Ellie, stressed out.

We end up exercising less. We stop playing. We sleep too little. We eat processed foods and have quick snacks, and life just keeps coming at us.

So, what happens as stress builds up inside of us? Well, lots of things, but in this story, Ellie's stress resulted in broken connections. She felt disconnected from Chase, Joe, and herself. When that happened, her *Angry Self* was standing by, waiting to defend and help her.

Ellie wanted to yell at Joe for not doing the dishes, not letting the dog out, and burying himself in a basketball game. She felt like going into the dining room, removing Chase's headphones, and letting him have a piece of her mind. In that moment, she was no longer in her Wise Woman Self. She had descended into her *Angry Self*. She had a weak connection to her HeartPrint.

She had another option besides blowing up. She could have just pushed everything down inside her. She had become an expert in doing that by then. She could have let that incident continue to feed some internal dialogue about how she was misunderstood, unappreciated, and unloved. That would have opened even more browser tabs and taken her further away from her HeartPrint. It would have chipped away at her connection to Joe, her connection to Chase, and ultimately her connection to herself.

There was a third option. Fortunately, Ellie remembered me and made space for me to appear by going outside, to a place that was soothing to her. She focused on her breathing, and then I got to help. She responded differently because she had turned toward me. I helped her turn away from responses that would have created more separation and choose a simple response that was *toward* the life she wanted to live. She strengthened the connection with me, and therefore her connection to her HeartPrint was reinforced by the choices she made.

Please allow me to share something called the Stress Curve. Maybe you will find it helpful.

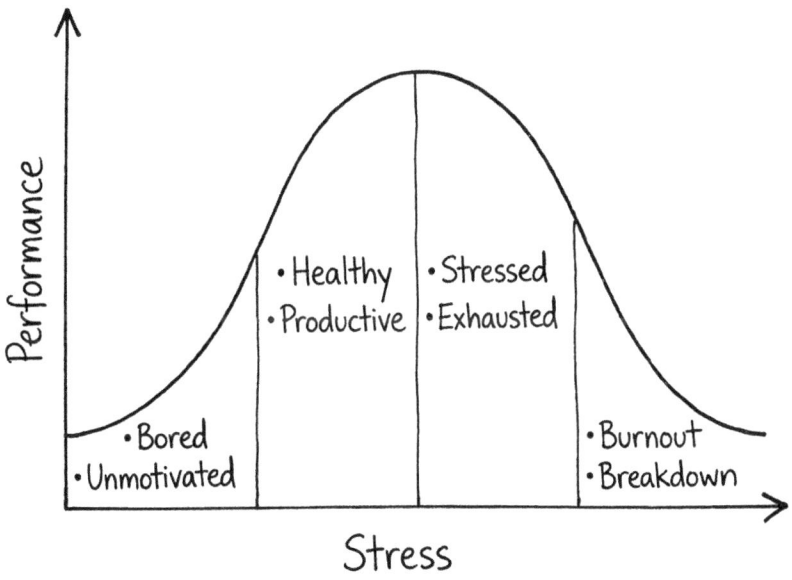

The Stress Curve

We have a couple of Americans, called Robert Yerkes and John Dodson, to thank for this. They created it all the way back in 1908, and it serves us well to this day.

It shows us that some stress in our lives is actually a *good thing*. When stress is absent or very low in our lives, as seen on the left-hand side of the curve, we become bored or unmotivated. There's not enough excitement or pressure, and we are under-engaged and underperforming in life.

Then there is the middle of the curve, where we have the right amount of stress. Yes, there is such a thing. All humans need a certain amount of stress to function well. When in this state, we perform at our best. We are focused, motivated, and interested. It's an ideal balance that serves us to accomplish the most we can. Sometimes you might hear about someone being "in the zone." That's what this is. We are powerfully connected to interesting work, and often our purpose and our relationships as well.

Then there's the bad kind of stress you can see on the right-hand side of the curve. When our stress gets too high, our performance starts to drop. We start feeling things like anxiety and pressure to perform. This can overwhelm us. It leads us to making mistakes, it impairs our decision-making, and it can end up with us burnt out and utterly exhausted. Our bodies react to defend us from threats. Stress hormones fill our bloodstream, and we are in survival mode. We even stop digesting food.

In this state of high stress, our decisions are not strategic; they are emotional. We just want the threat to be over, and we will do whatever it takes to immediately remove it. Unless these things are addressed, we can eventually slip into depression and full-on anxiety. Sleep becomes difficult. This kind of stress can even result in long-term illness.

Sounds pretty bad, right? Well, it is. It's no way to live our lives. We can continue for a while in this state, but it's like the Titanic heading toward the iceberg. It's only a matter of time before the crash happens.

One of the secrets of wisdom is an awareness of where you are on the Stress Curve. Recognizing that you are moving onto the wrong side of it will help you take the steps to avoid it. When we are living in our HeartPrint, we are in "the zone" about 80 percent of the time. No one can live in the zone all of the time, but with the help of your Wise Woman, you can be there most of the time.

Ellie didn't know anything about the Stress Curve in this story. But we got through the moment, at least. My hope for you is that, armed with this knowledge, you will be a step closer to creating a more secure bond with your Wise Woman and live closer and closer to your HeartPrint.

Ellie was able to negotiate that crisis. But the day-to-day life she was living wasn't giving her a life that felt good. She still wasn't ready for the challenging work needed to connect deeply and daily with her HeartPrint. The next few stories will share that difficult but ultimately triumphant part of her journey.

A Cup of Tea with Meg

Here, we learn about the Stress Curve and being able to work through a situation when our stress is high. We explore how stress can break connections. Here are some questions to consider:

- Where on the Stress Curve do you think you live most of your life? Which part of it do you make most of your decisions from?
- Is that serving you well? Would you like to change that?
- How easily can you recognize *in the moment* when your stress is on the curve? Are you able to figure out when someone else is on the wrong side of it?
- How does your stress break the connection with those around you?

The Second Part

Awakening → Remembering

The three parts of our emotional home

Another Letter from Elizabeth

Hello, friend,

The next few stories all happen in a short period of time. Ellie gets a chance to put into practice some things she learned from Joe's family. Then, Ellie and I connect and do a lot of work together. We are going to introduce the analogy of a staircase. It's something that helps explain Ellie's journey. I thought it might be helpful if I took a bit of time to explain the metaphor.

The Basement of Shadows

First, there's the Basement of Shadows. Yup, this is where your *Shadow Sisters* reside. It's where your life questions—hard things that have led to unanswered questions, pain, and emotional confusion—live. It's not a place you want to be in forever. However, as we will see, visiting it from time to time can be a good thing. In Ellie's Basement of Shadows, there are things like the hidden memories of her birth, the fall on the bicycle, the "that's not my baby" story, and so many other memories, rationalizations, and blaming of others. It's where our *Shadow Sisters* are the loudest, like our *Angry Self* and our *Blame-Shifting Self*.

The Cozy Landing

Then there's the landing. I call it the Cozy Landing because it's a very nice place to sit and do the work of growing, healing, and living. On the Cozy Landing, we organize our experiences, explore things, solve things, and plan things. In Ellie's imaginary landing, there is tea, a comfortable couch, a nice view, and plenty of writing materials. This is where we go to have quality time with our Wise Woman. We contemplate our HeartPrint, and we work through the myriad of life's complexities and relationships. We figure out how we don't just survive in this life but how we can live in harmony with our essence. It also includes having an everyday baseline of emotions like gratitude, appreciation, contentment, and satisfaction. There's a picture of it on the front of this very book.

The Beautiful Attic

Finally, there's the attic. It's called the Beautiful Attic because it's where we experience the very best moments of our lives. It includes moments that are transcendent and joyous. It also includes having easier access to the experiences of love, joy, peace, reverence, and enlightenment. Negative things, of course, can happen when we are in the Beautiful Attic, on the Cozy Landing, or on the stairs leading up to the Beautiful Attic, but we can handle them because we are connected to our Wise Woman and therefore our HeartPrint. We understand who we are and see our lives as part of a larger picture that affects generations to come.

Each of these places is connected by stairs. The stairs from the Basement of Shadows to the Cozy Landing are creaky, and can be scary and full of grief and pain. The stairs from the Cozy Landing to the Beautiful Attic are welcoming, inspiring, and expansive. They feel firmer under our feet, and there we experience emotions that range from neutral contentment to satisfaction all the way to unbridled joy.

I know I've mentioned this before, but thank you for suspending your disbelief in reading this book. There is a purpose to all of this. I hope by now, you've begun to form your own idea about how you and your Wise Woman relate to each other. I hope you are thinking about where you tend to "live" in your day-to-day life—whether it's the Basement of Shadows, the Cozy Landing, or the Beautiful Attic. And maybe how you move between those spaces. I hope I can create a bridge between you and your Wise Woman, so she and you can strengthen your relationship.

Our next story begins with Ellie and Joe after a really good day. Let's get started.

With more love,
Elizabeth

Chapter 7 · Age 42

the bedroom, Bluebell Lane, New Haven, Connecticut—a perfect party

Ellie climbed into bed next to Joe, who was reading a book.

"It seemed like Chase had a good time today," she said.

"Yeah," Joe replied, not looking up. "That marshmallow chocolate fountain was a real hit."

Ellie had planned and hosted a back-to-school party for Chase. He wasn't the most popular kid in the school because of his occasional outbursts, and Ellie had wanted to get the school year off to a good start. They'd invited a few of his classmates along with their parents, as well as Grace, her husband, and their daughter, Clara. Clara seemed to uniquely understand Chase, and they always had fun together.

"And I think the adults enjoyed themselves, too," Ellie continued, wanting affirmation from her husband.

Joe closed his book and turned more fully toward his wife, sensing that this was more than a casual debrief at the end of the day.

He thought for a moment, trying to remember when he had last felt like this. "It reminded me of the Poconos," he offered. It was a helpful answer for Ellie, who had wanted her husband's reassurance about her efforts.

"Yes!" Ellie exclaimed. "That's it! It had the same feeling."

Joe smiled.

"We never did anything like this growing up," Ellie continued. "I was so nervous hosting it. I mean, it's one thing to go to something like that. But planning it … well, that's a lot of pressure for me. I felt like I didn't know how to do it—like I was missing the manual."

Joe now understood where the conversation was going. The party seemed normal to him, but it wasn't for Ellie.

"The Rhodes family would have been proud," Joe said brightly, referring to his side of the family tree.

"Really?" Ellie replied, seeking reassurance, "Do you really think so?"

"It had everything," Joe said, thinking back on the details. "It was fun for the kids, fun for the grown-ups, and just the right amount of room for people to enjoy themselves."

"I talked to Charlotte last week," Ellie said, referring to Joe's talkative sister. "She suggested the chocolate marshmallow fountain."

"It was definitely a highlight," Joe said.

Ellie leaned over and kissed Joe's cheek. "Thanks, honey. That means a lot."

Joe put the book on the nightstand and turned off his light.

"Good night," he said. "You're a good mom, and that means a lot to me. Thanks, honey."

"Good night," Ellie answered, turning off her light. "Thanks. I'm glad we're in this together."

She closed her eyes and pictured Chase and Clara at the fountain, laughing as they dipped marshmallows into the chocolate. She took a moment to notice and appreciate the steps she had taken toward creating the life she had dreamed of as a child. Something inside her settled into place. She wondered if this was what Elizabeth meant by HeartPrint. She was proud of herself. Her last thought before she drifted off was that she must remember to tell Elizabeth the next time she saw her. It wouldn't always be perfect, she knew. But today shimmered like a small, perfect thing, and for now, that was enough.

Some days shimmer with small, perfect things.
And for now, that's enough.

From Elizabeth

I have found we can learn both from the good things that happen to us as well as the painful things. Ellie wasn't raised around a large, emotionally connected family. But through Joe, she was exposed to how a tight-knit family works. She learned that there is some design involved in forming connections, and it's more about providing opportunities for them through thoughtfulness than forcing them. Ellie was also learning how deeply satisfying it was to live in her HeartPrint, and to make her life on the outside match what she dreamed of on the inside.

It wasn't easy for her to take on organizing an event like this. She experienced much fear and uncertainty. But she researched and planned, and pulled it off. I was so very proud of her for being brave enough to give it a try. And she was rightfully pleased with herself.

That can be a tough thing for us, can't it? It seems like it's much easier to find fault with ourselves than to give ourselves credit. Taking pride in our accomplishments and our growth is a good thing. It builds confidence for other challenges we will face.

Ellie and Joe had also found some synergy. Although his HeartPrint was very different from his wife's, he had learned how to make room for her, and she for him. She had learned that speaking up and asking vulnerable questions helped him to connect with her. This wasn't something she could always do, as we will see. But when she did, it helped make things better.

For someone like Ellie, vulnerability was especially difficult. She had learned at an early age that exposing herself could bring judgment, ridicule, and anger. So it was a significant step forward for her to share so openly with Joe, as well as allow herself to be delighted by his response.

The foundation of their relationship was tested a little later. This is how the path to strengthening our HeartPrint goes—one step forward, two steps back. Our dear Ellie was about to confront a very difficult decision. I am so thankful I was there to help her.

She was about to find out about the Basement of Shadows and the Cozy Landing. I'm glad she got to visit the Beautiful Attic before it all began.

A Cup of Tea with Meg

We see Ellie at a high point in this chapter. She experienced what may seem like a small victory—hosting a successful party for her son, his friends, and their parents. But it wasn't small for Ellie. It was big. It was stretchy *and* nourishing. I'd like to invite you to explore these questions, so you can find your own threads to work on:

- Are there any things other people seem to find easy but you find difficult because of how you were raised or how your life has been, up to this point? What are they?

- Do you find it difficult to give yourself credit when you do something well? Why or why not? What might happen if you sat in the reassurance that you were successful, and could learn and do new things that brought you joy and satisfaction?

- Can you think of a time when you learned a big lesson from something *good* happening to you? What was it? Were you able to notice and appreciate yourself for your growth and learning? Could you try saying something complimentary to yourself now for the growth you have achieved?

Chapter 8 · Age 43

the Basement of Shadows, Bluebell Lane, New Haven, Connecticut—at the crossroads

Chase was now 10 years old and in the fifth grade. Most of the time, he and Ellie got along well. But there were times when she would get frustrated with him, mostly centered around his behavior at school. Chase would have outbursts that disrupted the class. They happened at home as well, but it was easier for Ellie to cope with those outbursts without the embarrassment that came from him acting out in public.

Chase would sense the frustration from his mother and withdraw. Ellie was unable to organize her complicated feelings about her son. After a day or two, things would return to something resembling normal. But each time it happened, the unspoken distance between them became harder to bridge.

Ellie and Joe had already been contacted twice during the first month of the school year. In the first incident, Chase had caused a commotion by continually making quacking duck sounds. Two weeks later, he had tossed a water bottle to the back of the classroom, where it had bounced off the wall and narrowly missed hitting another child on the head.

This was the subject of frequent arguments between Joe and Ellie. Ellie wanted to face the problem head-on, while Joe took a more passive approach. "It's just a phase," he would often say. Neither would give in, and the arguments usually ended in a stalemate with no solution. And, since they were both only focused on their son's symptoms, Chase was not getting the help he needed.

One of those arguments got particularly heated, so Ellie decided to sleep in the guest room. She awoke in the middle of the night, troubled. She groggily got out of bed and started wandering around. Her home somehow didn't feel familiar to her.

As she walked down a strange corridor, Ellie noticed a door she didn't recognize. She slowly opened it and saw some poorly lit stairs leading to a basement that she was sure wasn't a part of her house. Hesitating, Ellie felt a deep pull to start her descent and explore the basement. As she took the first step down, the stairs creaked. Stopping, she looked around. "Well, here we go," she said out loud.

She slowly continued. "I hope Elizabeth is down here somewhere," she mumbled quietly. She arrived at the bottom of the staircase and looked around the room. It was lit by a single, bare lightbulb that was swaying slightly, illuminating dusty, cobwebbed corners. The first thing she noticed was a poster on the wall. It read, "It's Not Your Fault," with an image of a city being destroyed by an earthquake. Ellie smiled.

Then she saw another poster that said, "At Least You're Safe Here." This one had an image of a safe falling from a window, heading toward an innocent bystander on the sidewalk.

Next, she saw some old boxes stacked on the floor. She walked over and read the writing on them. They were in her handwriting, scribbled in magic marker. One said "Dad." Another had "Mom" on it, with a line drawing of a woman in a bed and a speech balloon that said, "That's not my baby." Another box read "Boyfriends."

The basement felt strangely familiar to her. There was an old, beaten-up leather chair in the corner. She walked over and sat on it.

"Elizabeth?" she said aloud. "Are you here?" There was no answer.

She sat quietly for a moment, thinking about her argument with Joe. She wasn't alone for long. The *Shadow Sisters* came to help.

Chapter 8 • Age 43

Her *Angry Self* got things started as Ellie remembered the argument with Joe from earlier that evening and replayed it in her mind.

"He is so clueless," her *Angry Self* said. "He just wants everything to be *smooth*. He doesn't want to face the issue. What does 'growing out of it' even mean?"

Then she thought about Chase. "Why can't he just be a normal kid?" her *Angry Self* asked.

Her *Guilty Self* cursed her for the thought. "You are not a good mother. You should love him even though he's struggling," she said accusingly.

"It's Joe's fault," her *Blame-Shifting Self* said as she joined the party. "If he got more involved as a parent and a husband, this wouldn't be happening."

"And you try so hard," her *Victim Self* said to her. "And this is what you end up with? A tuned-out husband and a kid who throws things at school?"

Her *Victim Self* stepped fully into the spotlight.

"I don't get respect. I don't get appreciation. All I get is another list of things I'm supposed to do. And God forbid my mom or dad would ever lend a hand." She was tap-dancing furiously now, spinning stories as a way to protect Ellie from her fear that she had failed her son.

Ellie felt the uneasy satisfaction of self-justification. She sort of liked this place. There was no one to argue with her. This definitely felt better than just plain old helplessness. She found that the anger roused through victimhood had much more power.

Her thoughts were disturbed by clanking and clattering at the top of the stairs through the door she had left open. At first, this frightened her. Then she heard someone humming. It was definitely Elizabeth's voice.

Ellie stood up and walked to the bottom of the stairs. "Elizabeth, is that you?" she shouted.

Elizabeth appeared at the top of the stairs with a teapot in her hands. "Oh, my dear Ellie!" she said excitedly. "Please come up here at once. We have so much to talk about. I'm making tea."

Elizabeth disappeared, and the noise of preparation continued. Ellie looked around the basement, sighed, and walked slowly up the stairs. It was hard to leave. She noticed, as she took her first step, that she felt the hum of those downward-spiraling *Shadow Sister* thoughts trying to tug her back to the Basement of Shadows.

Ellie liked feeling the familiar friendship of her *Shadow Sisters*. She thought about staying there a bit longer, but the pull of Elizabeth's company was stronger, so she kept climbing. As she reached the top, she noticed she felt a bit better. She entered a new room that she didn't recognize. It could best be described as a Cozy Landing. There was a warm, dark green couch sitting underneath a beautiful loft-style window. Ellie realized that it must be morning, because there were streaks of sunlight painting the room.

Elizabeth was across the room with her back turned, preparing the tea. Ellie took in the rest of the room. In front of the couch, there was a strong, round wooden coffee table. On the table were two cups and a new-looking hardcover book. There was a bookshelf on the other side of the landing, filled with books Ellie didn't recognize. Besides the sunlight, the room was lit by tall lamps that emitted warm light.

She looked at Elizabeth, who was also dressed in pajamas. They had a soft floral print, like something out of a vintage catalog. Her feet were nestled into well-worn slippers that looked like they had stories of their own. Ellie was comforted to see the same pair of black-rimmed glasses.

"Sit, sit!" Elizabeth said. "I've made us some tea."

Ellie sat down on the couch, and Elizabeth filled the cups and set the beautiful teapot in the middle of the table. She then sat down next to Ellie and turned toward her.

"Where are we?" Ellie asked. "This is definitely not my house."

"Who knows?" Elizabeth answered, laughing. "The important thing is that we are here, and it is now. And isn't this place so *cozy*? Now drink your tea."

Ellie obediently took the cup and sipped.

Elizabeth continued. "I have it on good authority that this is going to be our special place for quite some time. No more of me showing up for a five-minute conversation. We are going to get to spend some *real time* together."

Ellie sipped again and looked out the window, taking it all in. She didn't recognize the landscape, but it looked the way she imagined the hills of Italy would look.

"First things first," Elizabeth said, picking up the book that lay on the table. "This is your *journal*." Ellie was surprised at how Elizabeth had said the word *journal*—with such pride and excitement.

"My journal?" Ellie asked.

"Yes," Elizabeth said, handing her the book. It was beautiful.

It was a large book and had a cotton-fabric hardcover. The edges of the pages were gilded. She opened it and saw paisley-patterned endpaper inside. The journal felt good to hold. The blank pages inside had substance. It also had three gold bookmark ribbons.

"And," Elizabeth continued, "I have a very special pen just for you."

She reached into a pocket in her pajamas and presented the pen with both hands. It was both slender and weighty—a fountain pen with a deep-blue lacquered barrel that shimmered when it caught the light. The nib glinted, sharp and delicate, as if it had been waiting only for Ellie's words.

"You are going to be amazed at the magic this pen and those pages will create," she said.

Ellie took the pen and opened the journal. There was nothing yet written in it. Of course, Ellie had heard of journaling, but she had never seen herself as the journaling type.

"What am I supposed to do?" Ellie asked.

"Easy. Write down your feelings," Elizabeth replied matter-of-factly.

"Write down my feelings?" Ellie asked.

"Yes, your feelings, darling. You know them, right? Your *big* feelings, your *small* feelings, your *middle* feelings," she said, winking.

"My feelings about what?" Ellie asked with a slight tone of annoyance.

Elizabeth sighed. "How about we start with Chase. What are your feelings about your son?"

"He's a great kid," Ellie replied, not putting pen to paper. "Those are my feelings about him."

Elizabeth let the words hang in the air. "Yes, he's a great kid," she finally replied. "But what are your *feelings* about him?"

Ellie thought about when she was in the basement and the conversation she'd once shared with the *Shadow Sisters*. She remembered specifically the thought, "I wish he could just be normal." Certainly, there was no way Elizabeth knew about that. And there was no way she would ever share that with anyone, not even her good friend.

Elizabeth broke the silence and said what was hanging in the air. "I sometimes just wish he could be normal," she said, looking over her teacup right into Ellie's eyes.

Ellie flushed with embarrassment.

"If you feel it, write it down," Elizabeth said gently, pointing to the page. "It's okay. What you are feeling is more common than you might think. You see, your feelings are important information. When you keep them inside, they keep growing. Then they come out at the worst possible times. It's much better if you get them out here, where it's safe. No one but you and I will ever see them."

Ellie placed the tip of the pen onto the first page of the journal but couldn't make a mark.

"What are you afraid of, darling?" Elizabeth asked.

Ellie realized she was truly afraid to express the feeling. To have the conversation in her mind was one thing. To openly share it was something quite different.

"Well, first of all, it's a horrible thought," Ellie said. "I mean, what kind of mother thinks that about her son?"

Elizabeth again left room for silence. "Who would feel that way about their son?" Elizabeth began. "How about countless mothers from countless generations in countless countries?" Elizabeth waved her hand each time she said the word *countless*. "Now, write. This is important."

"But what if someone—God forbid, Chase—would ever read this?" Ellie still wasn't writing.

Again, Elizabeth allowed Ellie's words to hang in the air. "It is a risk," she said, "but since you *have* those feelings about your son, don't you think Chase already feels that? He probably senses the separation between the two of you, and that could easily add to *his* pain and confusion. Wouldn't it be better for you to work through those feelings so you can bring out your best self as a mother? I would say it's riskier for you to feel it and not explore it. And you can't explore it until you admit you have it. Let's agree that there is no judgment in the journal. You need a place where you can express your truest feelings."

Ellie thought for a moment and decided to trust her friend. She wrote on the first page, "Sometimes I wish Chase would just be a normal kid."

She thought for a moment and stared at the word *normal*. She realized that was self-centered way to think about her son. Ellie dug deeper and wrote beneath the words, "Not *normal*. I want him to feel like he belongs. I want him to have good friends. I want him to be able to handle his life." It felt good to think about Chase this way. As she continued to write, the words came out faster and faster. It was as if something had burst open inside of her. She was flooded by a sense of relief that came from having somewhere to put everything. The pen on the page felt smooth and powerful. For the first time, Ellie felt a weight lift from deep inside her. In its place was a flicker of true hope.

"If you feel it, write it down,"
Elizabeth said gently, pointing to the page.

From Elizabeth

Ellie was reaching a point where she realized that what had got her to age 43 wasn't going to get her where she wanted to go in the next part of her life. This allowed Ellie and me to do some deep work together, which first involved discovering and holding space for her truest feelings and thoughts.

I had helped her before, but this time was going to be different. Her life had reached the point where she could either do some deep work or face some pretty catastrophic consequences.

Sometimes, it gets that way for us, doesn't it? We get really good at pushing things down, making things work, exploding when needed, and somehow surviving. But somewhere along the line, it's time. We either have to face our deepest feelings and thoughts head-on or start tearing things apart. (Sounds like a midlife crisis, doesn't it?) I suspect that if Ellie and Joe continued to travel further down this road, divorce would be somewhere on the horizon. Something had to give.

When Ellie descended into the Basement of Shadows, she felt helpless, hopeless, overwhelmed, and finally, angry. I was there on the Cozy Landing, waiting for her. I even called out to her. But she had to make the decision to come and join me. You see, your Wise Woman is never found in the basement. She will call out to you, sometimes multiple times, but you must decide to follow her voice.

This was the beginning of a profound change for Ellie. It was a time of discovery. She was beginning to recognize when she was in the Basement of Shadows (the *Shadow Sisters'* voices gave it away). She was in a different emotional place when she was on the Cozy Landing (exploring and working through her feelings without judgment). And finally, she began to recognize the Beautiful Attic, a place of clarity and empowerment.

She was discovering how my voice sounded and how she felt when she heard it. You see, it wasn't *wrong* that she had gone into the Basement of Shadows—that's the place where she could discover the next thing for her to focus on. It's just that she couldn't do any real work there.

Ellie was coming to understand she had to get to at least a neutral place (the Cozy Landing) where she could do the necessary work, like journaling. In this story, she saw she was in a downward spiral and the way out of it was to start climbing the stairs, where I was always waiting for her.

While Ellie was in the basement, she heard from her *Guilty Self* and her *Victim Self*. In addition, we met the *Inner Critic*, the *Blame-Shifting Self*, the *Anxious Self*, and the *Angry Self* earlier. Whew, that is a lot of voices! Are you friends with any of them? A way for Ellie to climb intentionally to the Cozy Landing was to start journaling. She got to that in this story, but you can start any time you like.

Let's explore our *Shadow Sisters* a bit more. I think we all have them. They are the parts of us that come to help us when we are on the wrong side of the Stress Curve (overstressed—see Chapter 6). Remember, these parts of us are just trying to be helpful. Usually, they are a younger version of us. They have learned to stand up for us. They know how to relieve the immediate tension we feel.

It's important to realize that our *Shadow Sisters* aren't usually parts of ourselves that have *grown up*. Mostly, they don't reflect our physical age. They act in our defense, but they often end up making things worse. They keep us stuck in a familiar cycle that doesn't allow us to grow into the next version of ourselves.

You see, our beautiful brains are like a stage, and only one part of us can be in the spotlight at a time. Whoever is in the spotlight directs our internal responses, words, and actions. It might be one of our *Shadow Sisters*. As we grow closer to our HeartPrint, our Wise Woman partnership will increasingly take center stage. A first step toward living a life where we access our Wise Woman's wisdom is the internal recognition of who stands in the spotlight. This is called *attunement*. The more attuned we become, the easier it becomes to shift to a space that is more helpful.

Our *Shadow Sisters* never actually leave the theater, but they can leave the spotlight where they call the shots. We don't actually *want* them to entirely leave. We need them. They have an important part to play in our lives. But if they are the ones under the spotlight onstage, things usually don't go well for us. When your Wise Woman is the star of the show, she points you toward your HeartPrint. When your Wise Woman is where she should be, your *Shadow Sisters* are at peace. Yes, you listen to them, but they don't get to take over your life.

When your *Wise Woman* is the star of the show, she points you toward your HeartPrint.

While in the basement, Ellie was very close to spiraling, which would have led to worse things for her. Although it felt good to ruminate, justify, and blame-shift, that wasn't a long-term solution. That wasn't going to get her where she wanted to go, which was to have a restored, good connection with her son, her husband, and herself. Unless Ellie did some deep work, she and Chase would keep butting heads. This would have led to further, and perhaps permanent, damage to their relationship.

So, it was high time for her to face and deal with the voices of the *Shadow Sisters*. It was time for her to move *toward* the life she wanted with her son. She was beginning to understand that staying in the Basement of Shadows and going through those spirals were moving her *away* from the life she wanted. She deeply desired to become more connected with Elizabeth and, therefore, her HeartPrint.

As humans, we all feel a shade better by ruminating, justifying, and arguing internally against the people who have hurt us. But we know, as Ellie was learning, it doesn't get us anywhere different in the long term. It was time for Ellie to do something new.

Ellie understood she was hurting Chase, her family, and herself. She had to choose differently this time. To do that, she had to get out of the basement. She had reached a crucial decision point, with long-term consequences. Ellie needed to learn to appreciate her son for all that he was. She wanted to become a mother who lived in harmony with him most of the time. It wasn't about perfection; it was about getting it right for the most part.

The first thing I had her do was to purposefully *externalize* her feelings. That was not easy. There was shame, guilt, and embarrassment associated with her feelings and thoughts. I helped her decide that the best way to move forward was to write them down. She could have chosen to speak her feelings aloud, like recording them on her phone, but writing them down so she could return to them seemed like the best choice for her in the moment.

Once she started writing, the feelings flowed into the journal. I had to really help Ellie not to be judgmental as she wrote them. She needed a warm, accepting space to get her feelings out and look at them honestly.

It doesn't matter if these feelings seem hideous. You see, it's normal for us to have immature, selfish, hurt, spiky, or angry feelings. It's easy to pretend we don't have them, but it's important to be honest with ourselves. Unless these feelings are processed and organized, they usually wind up spilling out onto those we love. It's far better they go into a journal where they can be honestly seen by us and our Wise Woman without hurting other people.

Getting feelings out allows us to get some emotional distance from them. We are able to see the thoughts and feelings through a different set of eyes. We can be more impersonal and analytical about what they are trying to show us. Instead of our feelings controlling us, expressing them allows us to be *curious* about them. When they are on the page, at a distance, we can see our emotions as though we have a 10,000-foot view.

I'm wondering if you've ever had a talk like this with your Wise Woman. Have you ever tried writing things down with the intention of working through them? Being deeply honest is hard, for sure. It takes creating a safe space for ourselves. It's almost like you have to tell yourself, "It's okay, I'll love you no matter what." *That* is the voice of your Wise Woman.

Here's something that might help. We talked before about the Stress Curve. This one is called the Feelings Wheel. It was first created in the early 1980s, and was the work of Dr. Gloria Willcox.

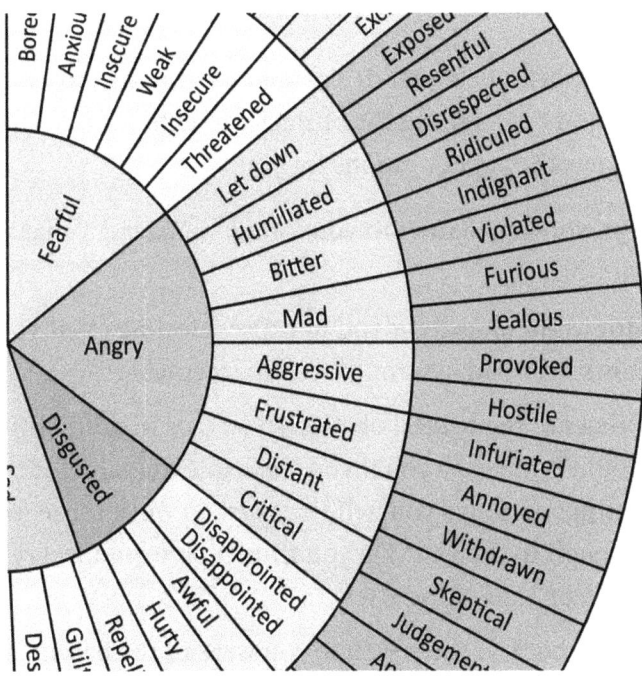

The Feelings Wheel: name it to tame it

Here's how it works. First, you start in the middle and ask yourself about a situation or a person. How do you generally feel about them? Next, go to the next circle. Can you relate to any of those feelings? Then follow the most present feeling to the next layer and choose one or more feelings, until you reach the outermost circle, writing down details of what you discover about your feelings.

Feelings can be complicated things. They are layered, nuanced, and overlapping. Sometimes there are good feelings and bad feelings mixed together about the same person or situation. I hope this wheel will help you to clarify your feelings. You might have heard the therapeutic saying, *Name it to tame it*. This is what we're working on when we use the Feelings Wheel.

Now that Ellie had started to externalize her feelings, she was ready for the next step. Our story will continue on that same night when we first shared the Cozy Landing together.

A Cup of Tea with Meg

This is an important chapter. It's about recognizing our *Shadow Sisters'* voices and overcoming the obstacles to externalize our feelings. Here are a few thought questions for you:

- Can you give names to your *Shadow Sisters*? What would they be?

- How difficult is it for you to express feelings that you might think are "bad," "wrong," or "unacceptable"?

- What are the biggest obstacles you face in doing this? What would it mean to you if you were able to really hear your feelings and give yourself the space to work those feelings through to the end? Do you think you would feel relief, hope, or something else?

- Think back to the last time you were in the basement. What feelings were underneath the *Shadow Sisters'* voices?

Chapter 9 · Age 43

the same night on the Cozy Landing, Bluebell Lane: truth, tea, and the journal

Sometimes I wish Chase would just be a normal kid.
Not normal. I want him to feel like he belongs. I want him to have good friends. I want him to be able to handle his life. What if he's lonely for the rest of his life?

Elizabeth sat quietly while Ellie looked at all of the words written on the first page of her new journal.

"Are you ready to explore your thoughts, wishes, and worries?" Elizabeth asked.

Ellie looked around. The sun had fully risen, and a beam of light shone on the bookshelf across the room. Both cups of tea on the table were nearly empty.

"I know what will help," Elizabeth said. "Let me fix us another cup of tea."

Ellie watched as she leaned forward and refilled their cups. She noticed the steady confidence in her movements and the gentle care in her hands.

Settling back onto the couch with her tea, Elizabeth said, "Come now, Ellie. Let's take the next step. How do you feel about *those* words on *that* page?"

After taking a sip, she repeated softly, "How do you *feel*?"

Ellie took a big breath and began.

"Sometimes I feel frustrated and angry at him. I feel a sense of resentment. And then I feel ashamed for having those feelings." She paused, letting the truth of it settle, then continued.

"When I let myself go down that road, everything feels heavier. I start imagining labels, classrooms that separate instead of include, medications that might change him in ways I don't understand. I worry about whether he'll feel like he fits in, whether he'll find friends who truly see him, whether he'll be able to meet life's challenges without feeling left behind. I wonder how long this season will last and what his future will be like."

"Lots of feelings," Elizabeth said quietly. "I understand every one of them. Those are troubling, for sure. Can you think of any other feelings?"

"What if Joe's right and this is just a phase?" Ellie asked. "Am I overreacting? I want to be a good mom to him. I'm so confused."

"Well, this part is kind of like playing golf," Elizabeth said. That got Ellie's attention. It was the one thing she and Joe did together, although lately not so much. "You have to take it one shot at a time," Elizabeth said.

Elizabeth handed Ellie a laminated piece of paper. It was the Feelings Wheel.

"Take a look at this," she said. "Pick one feeling you have about Chase."

Ellie located the word *angry* on the wheel. She looked at all the other feelings that were adjacent to it.

"It will help to write down your thoughts," Elizabeth said.

Ellie jotted down some of the words near *angry*.

- *Humiliated*
- *Frustrated*
- *Critical*

She added notes to each of them.

- *Humiliated—disrespected (school, teacher, Joe)*
- *Frustrated—annoyed (at Chase)*
- *Critical—dismissed (principal, Joe)*

Ellie put down the pen.

"Can I see?" Elizabeth asked.

Ellie sat back and handed the journal to her. Elizabeth ran her fingers over the words Ellie had written.

"What a great start!" she said proudly.

Ellie was unresponsive.

"Let's keep going. What else can you relate to?" Elizabeth asked, pointing again to the wheel.

Ellie said, "Fearful."

"Yes. Fear. There's a reason those are next to each other," Elizabeth said. "They are closely related. Why don't you write down some more *feelings*?" she said, exaggerating the last word with a smile.

Ellie explored her fearful feelings on a new page in the journal. As she wrote, she felt both good and bad at the same time. She felt a sense of relief when she wrote them down. She also felt guilty when she realized how many negative emotions surrounded her son, his school, and her husband, Joe.

Ellie got lost in thought, almost forgetting Elizabeth was there. She finished by writing the most honest thoughts she'd ever had in her life:

I hate that school. I don't think they understand Chase. What more can I do? He's a good kid. He plays on the soccer team. Why isn't he enough? I'm so worried.

How is he going to get through this year? I'm scared. What if this doesn't change?

Will he always struggle to find his place? Will I always be his safety net? Can I afford that emotionally, financially, spiritually?

Why does it look so effortless for other kids?

All I want is for my son to feel included, to walk into school without bracing himself, to be met with patience instead of judgment.

I feel dismissed by the school. I feel small. I can't change a whole society to meet the needs of my son.

When she had placed the last period in the journal, she looked up. Elizabeth had crossed the landing and was perusing the books on the bookshelf. Ellie sighed. She instinctively wanted to share what she had written with her Wise Woman.

"Well, it's official. I'm a complete mess," she said loudly enough for Elizabeth to hear.

Elizabeth walked over and sat down close to Ellie.

"You seem calmer," she said softly.

"I'm embarrassed about some of this ... well, actually, a lot of this," Ellie said, wafting her fingers over the book.

Elizabeth sat silently. "Read it for me," she finally said.

Ellie looked at the words on the page. Writing it was one thing; speaking it was another.

"It's just you and me," Elizabeth said. "No one else is here."

After a quick look around the landing to confirm they were alone, Ellie started to read. As she read, she experienced the emotions again. At times, she was angry. At times, she cried. Her tears dropped onto the pages.

Different parts of the *Shadow Sisters* spoke to her as she read. It was difficult for Ellie. It took her several minutes to get through the pages.

Elizabeth listened intently. At times, Ellie looked up from the page to see Elizabeth's face. There was no judgment, only kindness and acceptance.

When Ellie had finished, she breathed an even deeper sigh than before. She felt vulnerable and exposed. She slowly closed the book and looked at Elizabeth.

"What you have done is very brave," Elizabeth began. "I'm quite proud of you. Now, you haven't touched your tea. Shall I warm it up for you?"

Ellie shook her head.

"This is a *courageous* beginning," Elizabeth continued.

Ellie furrowed her brow. "It doesn't feel like it," she said. "All I've done is write some things down. All of the problems are there. This doesn't solve anything."

"Au contraire, mon amie," Elizabeth replied. "No more of that."

"No more of what?" Ellie asked.

"No more of this belittling and dismissing the important steps you are taking. I won't have it. You see, negative breeds negative, and positive breeds positive. It really is that simple. It's important to take the time and space to pat yourself on the back. I make a *regular practice* of it," she said with a contented smile.

Ellie nodded her head slowly. "Okay, okay, okay," she said. "I'm awesome because I'm so *bad*."

Elizabeth threw her head back and laughed. Ellie was unburdened enough to at least chuckle along.

Ellie picked up the journal, opened it, and glanced again at what she had written. "What do I do with *this*?" Ellie asked. She was surprised she felt something like a positive energy growing inside her.

"Well," Elizabeth slowly said. "What do you think? Give me your best guess."

"Well," Ellie said, emulating Elizabeth's tone, "I take it one shot at a time?" She tossed the notebook on the table and faced Elizabeth.

Elizabeth smiled. "Exactly. You can't solve everything at once. But each time you resolve one thing, you will have more energy for the next one." She took the book off the table and handed it back to Ellie.

"You have done a great job of exploring what it is you *don't want* for yourself. Read through what you have written. It tells us what you *don't want* in your life."

Ellie gave this some thought as she flipped through the pages yet again. "I never thought of it like that," she said. "Can you help me?"

"Of course," Elizabeth replied. "Try your best, and I'll help you."

"Okay, what I *don't* want is to feel overwhelmed by Chase's problems."

"Exactly. That's good. What else?" Elizabeth asked.

"I don't want to feel the tension between me and Joe. It's exhausting. And I guess I don't want to feel so resentful about *that* school. They just don't get it."

"All of those make sense," Elizabeth said. "Write all of those things down."

Ellie dutifully jotted them down on the page.

She thought for a moment and then added, "I don't want to feel so exhausted all the time."

As Ellie wrote this down, the positive energy from earlier grew a little. She looked up at Elizabeth as she finished. "Okay. Here's the list of things I don't want. Wow! There's a lot there. What comes next?" she asked.

"First, let's be thankful," Elizabeth replied. "Look how far you've already come."

Ellie nodded. "What comes next?" she repeated. She was anxious for the next part.

"You've done so much. Are you sure you want to keep going?" Elizabeth asked.

"I'm sure," Ellie replied confidently. "I can't leave it here."

Elizabeth smiled. "Alright, then. The next part is to take each of those things you *don't* want and ask what it is you want in their place. What is it that you *do want*?"

Ellie looked out the window. The sun was higher in the sky. She took a deep breath and started scribbling words in the journal. When she finished, she looked up and noticed that Elizabeth was dozing, leaning back on the couch. *She even looks like she's got it together when she's sleeping*, she thought.

On cue, Elizabeth opened her eyes and smiled. "Oh my! I drifted off. Have you finished?" she asked.

Ellie began to read. "Here are the things I want. I want to feel that everything is going to be okay. I want to feel like I'm a good enough parent to give Chase what he needs. I want to feel like I have the energy to deal with all of this. And I want to feel like Joe at least understands where I am coming from. I guess I want to feel supported." Ellie sighed.

"Wonderful!" Elizabeth said. "That is great work. Is there anything else?"

Ellie continued. "Yes, I want to feel like Chase's school is a good place for him to be."

"Wow!" Elizabeth said. "That's amazing. How does it feel to look at that page and see what it is you want in your life?"

Ellie sighed once more. "I don't know. It kind of feels empowering or something."

"Yes," Elizabeth said. "That's exactly it. You are in charge of your life, and you can decide what you want from it."

Ellie smiled slightly. She felt better.

Elizabeth continued. "There's one more thing, if you're up to it."

Ellie nodded. She was ready for whatever Elizabeth might say.

"Your final mission, should you decide to accept it, is to write down what you can *do* to feel the ways you want to feel," she began. "You see, you have more power over your life than you think. Your contentment is much more under your influence than you might realize. Even though others may contribute to your pain and confusion, you can choose to move *toward* your Cozy Landing, find me, and reconnect to your HeartPrint. No one can stop you from doing that."

"My HeartPrint?" Ellie asked. Elizabeth had mentioned her HeartPrint once before, but Ellie didn't understand what it meant.

Elizabeth smiled. "Yes, my dearest, your *HeartPrint*. It's who you are—your essence. It's who you were made to be. To borrow a Dr. Seuss quote, 'It's the *youiest* version of you.' Which means it's a wonderful version of you. Your HeartPrint has always been here, and what has separated you from it is the act of being a human living a human life. I'll help you find it. It's a *wonderful* place to live."

"So, do you live in your HeartPrint?" Ellie asked.

Elizabeth chuckled. "Well, I do *most of the time*. I don't think it's possible to do it all the time. It's a journey that never ends," she said, sitting back on the couch and looking up at the ceiling. "And today, we will come up with a plan for you, if you want."

"I want to live in my HeartPrint," Ellie said with conviction.

"Then let's get to work!" Elizabeth said. "Write down some things you can do to move toward the life you want to live. Go through each of these things," she said, pointing to Ellie's list on the page.

Ellie looked at the first line.

"I want to feel everything is going to be okay. I want to feel like I'm a good enough parent to give Chase what he needs."

She thought about how she could move toward that feeling. She remembered that Grace had shared about getting professional help when her father had passed away.

"Maybe I could find a therapist who specializes in kids. Maybe they could help me understand how I can best help Chase," she said, looking to Elizabeth for approval. "I could find out if this is just a temporary thing or if maybe there's something else going on with him, like a medical issue."

Elizabeth winked at her. "You are on the right track. Write that down. Excellent. Keep going."

Ellie jotted down some notes. Her eyes went to the next thing on the list.

"I want to feel like I have the energy to deal with all of this."

Ellie realized that taking care of her energy had been far down on her list. All of her energy had been focused on work, Chase, and Joe. She thought about what made her feel more energetic. She remembered how good she'd felt when she'd spent time with Grace. She thought about the walks she used to take that had fallen by the wayside.

"I need to make time for Grace," she said confidently. "And I need to start walking again."

"That's great," Elizabeth said. "Write it down. Those are things you could do any time you like."

Ellie wrote and then looked back at her list of things she wanted in her life.

"I want to feel like Joe at least understands where I am coming from. I guess I want to feel supported."

She was gaining momentum. "I can ask Joe to sit down and have a conversation about Chase, instead of waiting for the next fight. We are not on the same page."

Ellie didn't wait for Elizabeth's response. She turned to the last item.

"I want to feel like Chase's school is a good place for him to be."

"I can go to the school with some ideas about how we can help Chase. If they can't work with me, I can research some other schools," Ellie said, finishing the writing in her journal.

She sat back and looked at her work. "And, I guess writing this stuff down can become a habit," she said, tapping the pen on the notebook. Ellie closed the journal. She was done. "Thank you," she said. "Thank you for your help."

"You've come so far in such a short time," Elizabeth replied. "You have a *plan*! Just think, a couple of hours ago, you were down there." Elizabeth eyed the staircase to the basement.

"I don't think I ever want to go back there," Ellie said.

"Well, the basement is an interesting place," Elizabeth answered. "You definitely don't want to live there. However, from time to time, it's not a bad place to visit. It's a great place to learn. The secret is not *staying* down there. I'm actually quite grateful for all I have learned from visiting the basement."

Ellie felt better than she had in a long time. She had a way forward. She felt empowered. She had a plan. The two of them stood up. "I love you," Elizabeth said softly.

"Thank you," Ellie said.

"Now, off to bed with you. I think it's getting dark again," Elizabeth said.

Dusk was settling over the hills. Ellie realized the whole day had somehow passed. Confused but happy, she made her way back to the guest room and fell asleep.

"You have more power in your life than you think."

From Elizabeth

It's hard to say how long that time on the landing lasted for Ellie and me. At the time, it felt like a day and a night. Looking back on it, it might have been weeks or even months. I guess it doesn't really matter. What matters is what happened there. I've learned that growth and understanding can sometimes come in spurts, and other times, more slowly. Either way, our time together was remarkable, and Ellie left with a new way to look at life.

It was so *helpful* for Ellie to start off by sitting with her feelings without judgment. It really was the first step toward strengthening the connection with her HeartPrint. She had come unstuck by disrupting the pattern. Before, it was a cycle of bad feelings: Her *Shadow Sisters* would come to her defense, the situation would fade away, and she would eventually return to life. But each time the cycle repeated, she found herself further from her HeartPrint. On the Cozy Landing, I helped her to handle her feelings differently.

You see, your HeartPrint is the fullest expression of who you are. Each time you move away from it, you lose access to the full growth and potential that you have. You will be happiest when you live mostly in your HeartPrint.

Each time you move away from your HeartPrint, it feels wrong, itchy, or painful. You can end up spending a lot of time in your Basement of Shadows, which cannot move you toward the life you dream of. But every time you climb the stairs and stay on the Cozy Landing, you can access your inner wisdom to process your experiences and move toward the life you want to live. You have access to a fuller expansion of who you really are.

There will be times when you have strong negative feelings while you are on the Cozy Landing. Ultimately, it feels nourishing and good, like you've been able to organize everything into the right place. The longer you can stay on the Cozy Landing, the more your life will match the HeartPrint that belongs only to you.

Your HeartPrint is like a seed. A lot of seeds look alike. But when they are planted and come out of the ground, each one produces a different kind of plant. One might be an azalea bush. Another might be an orange tree. Each seed becomes something unique and beautiful. Your HeartPrint contains the full expression of who you really are, and you will discover it bit by bit.

Each of us can become a full expression of self—what we were meant to be. That's how we will feel the best about ourselves. Then, at the end of our lives, we can look back and be proud of the life we have lived.

I hope you noticed how I helped Ellie meet her big feelings without shame. Our embarrassing emotions need to be met with compassion and understanding. That's something we seem to do better with others than ourselves. Somehow, we are able to hold empathy for others' feelings but not our own. I would often ask Ellie, "What would Grace say about your feelings?" Or, "If Grace confided feelings like this to you, how would you respond? Would you be able to extend that same grace to yourself?" That would help her switch her perspective.

It started with Ellie writing down her negative feelings. This is always a good place to begin. It has to be honest. It takes some thought, time, and energy. You might find yourself avoiding doing this. If so, that is a sign of your *Shadow Sisters* having a strong hold on you. Maybe you need to finish feeling those feelings before you can begin the climb to the Cozy Landing. That is okay. Just don't live in the basement for too long, because it will hurt you more than you realize.

This process led to helping Ellie realize that what she had written down was a list of things she did *not* want in her life. Next, she embraced that moment of self-awareness.

Then, it was time to flip it around. Instead of focusing on what she *didn't* want, I asked her what she *did* want. That was an important step. It gave her clarity. She started to become *unconfused*. (Is that even a word?)

Finally, we came up with a plan to help move *toward* the life she wanted to live. There were conversations to have, research to be done, and walks to be scheduled.

As her Wise Woman, I was helping her understand she had *control* over her life. Life wasn't just happening *to* her; she had choices. It's something called *agency*. It's when we understand that we are responsible for our own happiness and we can map out our own destiny. It is empowering.

As she processed her feelings outside of her beautiful brain and onto her journal paper, where she could see them from more of a distance, some of her browser tabs began to close. This gave her a boost of energy and a feeling of hope. For the first time in a long time, she allowed herself to feel excited about the future. She had a sense of order and progress in her life.

Let's talk about one of the most prominent *Shadow Sisters*, the *Inner Critic*. When Ellie started writing out her darker feelings, her *Inner Critic* almost took her back to the basement. As I've said before, this *Shadow Sister* was only trying to help her. Her *Inner Critic* knew that as long as Ellie was focused on how much of a failure she was, at least she wouldn't have to face the disappointment of getting her hopes too high.

The *Inner Critic* is built within us from an external source—people like our primary caregivers in our early years, and our peers and teachers in our childhood years. This part is not without valuable information. But most often, she brings it to us in a way that is overly harsh and not helpful to our situation. This is where your Wise Woman can step in and help you grow from the information your *Shadow Sister* brings, without letting it become debilitating.

Our *Inner Critic* can make an appearance when an old friend or sibling teases us about something from when we were growing up. Instead of amusement, we feel a flash of anger or deep embarrassment. Consider this an invitation to turn *toward* the feeling and not react emotionally. Perhaps we could become curious about the emotion and recognize that the feeling is giving us vital information about ourselves. Perhaps there is something there to attune and attend to.

Ellie was 43 when we had this extended time in the Cozy Landing. I have found that the decade of our 40s can be tough. There's a reason the term "midlife crisis" has found its way into our vocabulary. Somewhere around this age, we begin to deeply understand that we are finite and we have lived about half of our lives. We've accumulated a lot of experiences, both good and painful. We know what it means to live in our HeartPrint and out of it.

This is often a time when we deeply consider who we want to be and how we want to spend what remains of our lives. We have to wrestle with old hurts and pains from our past and begin to work through those feelings.

Most of the time, there are a lot of people who depend on us, from our spouses or partners to our children, our parents, our community, our workplace colleagues, and beyond. Things get real in our 40s. They can be complex and complicated years. They can also be absolutely wonderful.

Often, we are still working on building a strong relationship with our Wise Woman during this time. Maybe you've noticed that she kind of comes and goes. Maybe she feels fleeting to you at times. Maybe this is the quietest she has ever been.

The more you get to know your Wise Woman, the more she can help. The more you actually *become* her, the more you will understand your *Shadow Sisters* and be able to distill valuable wisdom from them. And you will move ever closer to living in your HeartPrint most of the time.

A Cup of Tea with Meg

Whew! We covered a lot in this part. I hope it was helpful. It gives you a pattern for how to work through your big feelings, one by one. There are many questions I could ask, but here's a place to start:

- Can you think of one big feeling in your Basement of Shadows that you would like to explore?

- Take the time to write down the feeling and follow these steps:
    - Write it down and sit with it without judgment.
    - What is it you *don't* want?
    - What is it you *do* want?
    - What can you do to move toward what you want?
- What percentage of the time do you feel connected to your Wise Woman? There's no right or wrong answer; there's only the truth. Then you can choose what to do next.
- What does feeling a sense of *self-agency* mean in your journey toward your HeartPrint? How might you add 10 percent more of this sense of autonomy to your daily life?

Chapter 10 · Age 43

Edgewood Park walking trail, near Bluebell Lane—a root, a fall, a twisted ankle

The next morning, after the extended time with Elizabeth in the Cozy Landing, Ellie awoke, trying to make sense of everything that had happened. She felt both energetic and curious. Chase called out from upstairs, "Mom, I can't find my socks!"

"I'll be right there," she shouted back. She was surprised to find herself eager to help her son. She felt differently about him, like her connection to him was somehow cleaner.

After helping Chase, she dove into the day. Joe had left early for work, but Ellie had a late start. She fixed Chase's breakfast and got him off to school. She looked at him as he walked out the door. Ellie quietly noticed that her complicated feelings, like worry, fear, and anger toward Chase from the days and weeks before, were starting to be replaced with something more like hope.

Once alone, her mind returned to the previous night. She wondered if the journal she had started was actually real. If so, where would it be? She went back to the guest room where she had slept and started looking around. Eventually, she looked under the mattress, and there it was. She sat on the edge of the bed, opened it, and began to read all of her thoughts from the night before. Ellie finally arrived at the last page. On it, there was a list of actions for her to take.

1. Find someone to help Chase (professional)
2. Set up a time to meet with the teacher and principal (proactive)
3. Get some help for myself
4. Research other schools (if needed)
5. Spend time with Grace
6. Talk to Joe
7. Start taking hikes

Ellie looked through the list. She decided that the first thing she would do was text Grace. "Missing you. Coffee this week?" she wrote, knowing that even though Grace lived 30 minutes away, she was always up for coffee and a talk. She put a check next to number five.

Glancing at her phone and realizing she only had 30 minutes before getting ready for work, she decided to tackle number three. She opened her laptop and typed in, "Mental health professionals family specialty near me." She scrolled through the results. *Whew,* she thought. *How do I choose?*

She typed again, "Mental health professionals to help parents with difficult children near me." This time, she noticed a listing that said, "Best Pediatrician in the City." She took some time to research the provider, and a few minutes later, she had an appointment set. She closed her laptop with a satisfied smile and got ready for work. She felt more enthusiastic, energized, and thankful than before.

When she arrived at work, she made a schedule for walking four times a week. She had a productive day and drove home, playing out the conversation she wanted to have with Joe about Chase. She was on a roll.

She walked into the kitchen where Chase was sitting at the table, doing homework. "How was your day, love?" she asked.

Chase looked up, unconsciously measuring his mother's mood. When he saw the smile on her face, he smiled back.

"Good," he said, returning his pencil to paper.

"Well, I had a great day, too," Ellie said, sitting down next to him. Chase looked up again.

"Can I tell you about it?" she asked.

"Sure," Chase replied, putting down his pencil.

"Well," Ellie said, "It was actually great. I'm having coffee with Aunt Grace on Friday, and I'm going to start my walks again tomorrow."

"Cool," Chase said. "Miss Keene is *funny*," he continued, changing the subject to what was on his mind.

"Funny? How is Miss Keene funny?" Ellie asked warmly about Chase's teacher.

"Well," Chase said, "instead of *spaghetti*, she always says, 'pasghetti.'" He giggled.

"Pasghetti?" Ellie repeated. "I thought that's what it was called!"

"No, Mom, it's pasghetti … I mean spaghetti."

They both laughed.

"I like her, though," Chase said. "She always has a pencil if you forget yours."

Ellie smiled. "Sounds like she pays attention."

Chase shrugged, already looking back at his worksheet. "I guess."

Ellie rubbed Chase's head, got up, and started fixing dinner.

She was finishing when Joe came through the door. They looked at each other, both remembering the fight from the night before and wondering who would be the first to speak.

"Hey," Ellie finally said.

And then quietly, out of Chase's earshot, she added, "I'm sorry about last night."

"Yeah, me too," he replied.

Ellie finished setting the table. "Let's eat," she said.

※ ※ ※ ※

The next several days followed suit. Ellie started to implement her new plan. She went on her walks and had a great time reconnecting with Grace. Although she and Joe hadn't had a meaningful conversation, she moved back into their bedroom. She asked if they could go out to dinner that Saturday, where she planned on talking to him about how they could work together with Chase.

Most days, she would steal away and work on her journal. She enjoyed those times. The book had become a symbol of the work she was doing. The pen was exquisite, and the paper was special. She would explore her feelings without judgment, figure out what she wanted and didn't want, and come up with a plan. She was gaining momentum toward a life that felt *good* to her.

Early one morning before Joe and Chase were awake, she sat quietly, sipping coffee and exploring the latest entry in her journal. A beam of morning sun shone in, just in front of her. It crept up and warmed her knee. She saw the dust particles in the air. She sat back, smiled, exhaled, and simply enjoyed a small, precious moment of the day.

Saturday came, and Ellie slept in. When she woke, she saw that Joe's place in the bed was empty. She got up, made herself a cup of tea, went to the guest room, pulled out her journal from under the mattress, and sat down in a chair next to the bed. She opened it to a blank page and started to write about the conversation she planned to have that evening with her husband.

Her first thought was from her *Angry Self*. It raised a thought about his cavalier attitude. She thought back to all of the times he'd been dismissive of her fears about Chase and noticed a churning in her stomach. Ellie took a deep breath and made room for the thought. She went through her process.

"What *don't* I want?" she wrote.

Underneath, she jotted down:

Facing this alone
Being in competition with Joe

Then, following what Elizabeth had taught her, she wrote, "What *do* I want?" underlining the word *do*.

Be a team
Him and me against the world

Figuring out Chase together
Joe to understand where I'm coming from

Finally, she wrote "The Plan."

Give Joe a chance to respond differently
Present my thoughts kindly
Make room for his opinion

She closed the journal, bookmarking the page, and let out a deep sigh. Her hopes were high.

As she was dressing for her walk, she looked out the window and noticed that Joe's car was gone. *Probably running errands*, Ellie thought. Tying her shoes, she went down the stairs through a silent house. She stepped outside into a brilliant, crisp Saturday morning, put in her earbuds, and began her walk.

She followed her usual route that led to Edgewood Park. Ellie particularly enjoyed the part of the hike that led through the trees and on the dirt path instead of concrete. As she started that part of her journey, her mind drifted to Chase.

Her *Anxious Self* started asking questions.

"Will this really work?" the *Shadow Sister* said in a tone of voice that troubled Ellie.

"Will things really be different? Do you really think you can talk to Joe about this without getting into a fight?"

Her *Inner Critic* joined the conversation. "I don't think you can really change. You'll mess this up just like your mom did with you. What if you're a bad mom, and always will be?"

"It's probably too late anyway," her *Guilty Self* said. "You've already messed it up too much. You've already damaged Chase. He's never going to be any better. This is all just a pipe dream."

※ ※ ※ ※

Ellie's heartbeat quickened as she ruminated on these thoughts. She didn't understand. Why here? Why now? She felt a knot in her stomach. Her hands began to sweat, and she went over the top and onto the wrong side of the Stress Curve.

Distracted, she looked up in frustration. She let out a small groan.

Just then, she tripped over a large root, fell, and landed with a thump on her side. "Ouch," she said out loud. "That hurts."

Wet dirt and leaves covered her from ribcage to knee. Trying to stand, she had trouble putting weight on her injured foot. "Great," her *Inner Critic* said. "Just like you. You never pay attention. You're always in a hurry, and *this* is what happens. What a loser."

She sat back down on the ground, panicking a little, and rubbed her ankle as the chill of her wet clothes hit her flesh. She thought about calling Joe, but decided instead to try to hobble home. Her knee was scraped, and her ankle was swelling, but she managed to limp home. Ellie opened the door and made her way to the couch. The pain was intense.

"Chase!" she said in a loud voice. "Chase!" she shouted louder. She heard a door open upstairs.

"Mom?" Chase shouted, "Are you okay?"

"I twisted my ankle on my hike," Ellie said. "Could you get me some ice?"

Chase came down the stairs and headed toward the kitchen. He repeated his question, "Are you okay, Mom?"

"I think so. But I twisted it pretty bad."

Before Chase could return with the ice, Joe walked through the door. He saw Ellie sitting on the couch, rubbing her ankle. "What happened?" he asked.

"I was going on my walk and tripped over a root," Ellie said with a pained look on her face.

Joe came over and sat next to her on the couch. Chase arrived with the ice, and Joe put it on her ankle. "Sorry," Joe said.

"I can be so stupid," Ellie said. Her *Inner Critic* was on center stage. Elizabeth was nowhere to be found.

"It looks like a sprain," Joe said. "And your knee is kind of scraped up."

"Yeah," Ellie said, her eyes filling with tears. "I'm a mess."

"Sorry this happened, Mom," Chase said, kneeling down and touching the scraped knee.

"Ouch!" Ellie said angrily, "Don't touch it!"

Startled, Chase withdrew his hand quickly and looked up at his mother, eyes wide with shock. "Sorry," Ellie offered weakly. "It just really hurts."

Chase stood up, not sure what to do. His heart, full of fear from his mother's reaction, pounded.

"Maybe go back to your room," Joe said quietly, "I've got this."

Chase quietly ascended the stairs, angry with himself for doing the wrong thing.

Joe rearranged the ice pack. "Would you like some water?" he asked.

Ellie nodded.

When he returned, he said, "Sorry to bring this up now, but there's something I need to talk to you about."

"What?" Ellie asked without meeting his eyes.

"Well, we got another notice from the school yesterday," Joe said quietly.

"What?" Ellie's voice was raised. "Why didn't you say anything?" Her *Angry Self* had now taken center stage.

"Well, I was going to talk to you about it at dinner tonight," Joe said. "But that doesn't look like it's going to happen."

"Tell me," Ellie demanded.

"Same old stuff," Joe replied. "This time, it was on the playground. Something about throwing sand in a girl's face. The principal wants to meet on Friday."

Ellie's *Blame-Shifting Self* thought, *If he says it's just a phase, I'm going to lose it.*

On cue, Joe said, "I think it's something a lot of kids go through. I think he will grow out of it."

"He *won't* grow out of it," Ellie said angrily. "He needs help. *We* need help."

Joe sat there, not saying anything.

"You always do this," Ellie began. Her *Shadow Sisters* of blame-shifting, frustration, and anger were singing in harmony. She looked at Joe with the kind of corrosive contempt that can destroy a relationship.

Ellie was shouting. "You want to sweep everything under the carpet and pretend there's not an issue. You ignore, ignore, ignore. Can't you see this problem is getting worse? What's it going to take for you to *wake up*?"

"That's not fair," Joe said. "You overreact."

"*Overreact*!?" she said loudly. "He's kicking desks, making duck calls, throwing water bottles, and now sand? I overreact? What the heck, Joe?"

Her critical, lonely, and overburdened *Shadow Sisters* joined in. "I feel like I'm all alone. If anything ever gets done, it's me doing it. If it were up to you, nothing would ever happen. Sometimes I wonder what else is going on with you."

"What's that supposed to mean?" Joe asked incredulously.

"It means you aren't here for this family. Where were you this morning?" she asked. The stage was getting crowded with each of her *Shadow Sisters* vying for the spotlight.

"Where was I?" Joe replied. "I was looking at a set of used golf clubs," he said sheepishly.

"Well, good for you," Ellie said sarcastically. She was well into the Basement of Shadows. "Because that's what this family needs. A new set of golf clubs."

Joe started to say, "Golfing is something we do together. What you are saying is totally unfair." Instead, he stood up, shook his head, and walked silently into the kitchen.

Ellie's cell phone buzzed. It was a text message from the "Best Pediatrician in the City."

"Your appointment has been rescheduled," it began. She didn't bother to read the rest of it. She threw the phone onto the floor, cracking the screen. She put her hands on her head and ran her fingers through her hair. Her ankle was throbbing, and her knee was burning. Her wet and dirty clothes had started to stain her couch. She blurted out an awkward whimper. Ellie couldn't hold it in any longer and began to sob uncontrollably, the kind of ugly crying where it feels like even your pain dribbles down your chin.

She heard Chase's door close upstairs. *Did he hear all of that?* she wondered, as she cursed herself.

She was defeated, discouraged, and angry. All of the gains she had made seemed to have been lost in the course of an hour.

"Ouch," she said out loud. "That hurts."

From Elizabeth

Our memories aren't always broad and sweeping. Sometimes they are specific moments—snapshots of words said or actions taken. This was one of those times.

In just a few moments, all of Ellie's progress seemed to disappear. All of her good intentions were thwarted. All of her hard work seemed to amount to nothing. It felt even worse than her not doing anything at all. At least if she hadn't tried, she wouldn't have failed.

It was very hard at that moment for Ellie to be anything but negative and discouraged. I understand. When we get on the wrong side of the Stress Curve, it's nearly impossible to take a step forward unless we regulate ourselves first.

It didn't feel like it at the time, but this incident was just another step in Ellie's journey toward her HeartPrint. It's rarely a straight line. She was still learning to recognize her patterns and build her muscle of attunement, and right now, she wasn't able to think clearly in the moment. She needed to reset, like she had done back in the apartment, before she could take any meaningful action.

One negative thing led to another. Our beautiful brains have that kind of bias. If given the choice, we are programmed to focus on things like danger and threats. It's what kept our ancestors alive in the savanna. This negativity bias has followed us into modern times.

For instance, there are twice as many words in the English language for "negative" as there are for "positive." On the positive side, we have words like *happy, joyful,* and *excited.* On the negative side, there are many more words. There are words like *anxious, angry, frustrated, miserable,* and *despairing.* As humans, we don't feel the need to investigate good feelings in the same way as we do negative ones.

So it takes work and time for us to settle in and have our Wise Woman at center stage most of the time. Each day has its share of good and bad. Most of our lives are somewhere in the middle. But since we have a natural attraction to the negative, it takes a conscious effort and attunement not to live there.

Without conscious effort, we gravitate toward the Basement of Shadows. The stronger the connection between you and your Wise Woman, the more you are able to create space in the moment and see negatives in a different light. You discover that "bad" events you have experienced in your life (even ones that are not your fault) are not inevitably linked to bad or negative outcomes. Instead, you become curious about these feelings and experiences and start to wonder what they may have to teach us about what it is you *don't want*. These experiences don't have to define us. They can *inform* us.

The *Shadow Sisters* take center stage as the *Wise Woman* waits in the wings.

Ellie had to learn this lesson. She was moving forward until she hit the hurdle of the dreaded tree root. It overwhelmed her newly found way to process negative feelings, and it disrupted her progress.

And she was doing so well! I loved that she noticed the beautiful ray of sun that warmed her leg. As she left for her walk, she breathed in the fresh air, grateful for a gorgeous spring day. She noticed how much easier it was to walk as it became a habit, and she praised herself for her progress. She smiled and greeted the other walkers along the way. She was walking close to her HeartPrint and had positive emotional momentum.

And then it happened. An anxious thought about Chase led her to doubt herself. That led to an angry thought about Joe. She turned her attention to the lack of resources at the school. She started ignoring her environment, got distracted, and tripped. When she landed on the ground, hurt, her *Shadow Sisters* began to take center stage.

Part of her challenge was that we, as women, face unrelenting standards every day. There is just so much expected of us. It's easy to spend our day trying to tick all the boxes to meet these standards. We are at once supposed to be good wives, good mothers, good daughters, good sisters, good friends, and good parents. That's just in our personal lives! There are even more expectations at work. It is very hard to feel successful and even harder to feel content and satisfied and that everything is good when there are so many places for us to fall short of the mark.

It's easy to compare ourselves to others. Everyone else seems to handle their lives so much better than we do. We criticize ourselves for operating at 7/10 since others are apparently handling their lives at 9/10. In this frame of mind, it's a short walk to the Basement-of-Shadows.

But it doesn't have to be this way. Instead, I invite you to notice and appreciate yourself in specific ways. If you have joined Ellie in journaling, take some time to write out good things about yourself. Perhaps it's something as simple as today, when you sat without your phone, ate breakfast, and let yourself breathe for five minutes. You simply enjoyed the silence of connecting with your HeartPrint for a few minutes. That is no small thing.

Treating yourself in this way isn't an afterthought or a meaningless add-on. You might be tempted to dismiss all of this "think positive" stuff as trivial. I admit it has become a trite and diluted idea in our culture. It's so overused that it's easy to miss a deeper truth. I'm not talking about some false narrative that we tell ourselves. I'm talking about genuinely noticing the good and nourishing experiences we have access to each day and how we are making progress toward a life that feels good. This kind of effort will yield true results and move us toward the life we want to live.

Being intentional like this is about focusing on where our attention goes and our energy flows. When we actively notice the places in life that are authentically good for us, we make progress. It gives us something to build on. I encourage you to give it a try.

Anyway, let's not leave poor Ellie with her swollen ankle all by herself, alone on the couch and in a Basement-of-Shadows frame of mind. If she ever needed me, it was then. I was there on the Cozy Landing, waiting for her to come and take the next steps toward me, and therefore, her HeartPrint.

A Cup of Tea with Meg

Joe and Ellie have a nasty fight in this chapter. Let's take a few minutes to think about Ellie. Here are some questions to consider for your journaling:

- How did things escalate so quickly between Ellie and Joe? Can you remember a time when this happened to you? What do you wish you had done differently to interrupt the downward spiral?

- How do you relate to the idea that women face unrelenting and sometimes unreasonable expectations in our culture?

- How often during the course of a day do you truly, genuinely, notice and appreciate the good you have built and the wonderful moments you have?

Chapter 11 · Age 43

the return to the Cozy Landing—attunement and a way forward

Ellie sat on the now-stained couch alone. Her ankle and knee throbbed. Joe had left, and she had been cruel to Chase. She was utterly discouraged.

"Elizabeth?" she said out loud with desperation in her voice. There was no answer.

She closed her eyes, waved her hands like a magician would, and said, "Elizabeth, appear!"

She looked around. There was no Elizabeth.

I need you, she thought to herself. *Where are you?* And then with more fervor, *WHY AREN'T YOU HERE!?*

Ellie took a deep breath. And then another. And then another. Some time passed as her body regulated and her physiology dropped back into a steadier zone. As it did, she became clearer about what she needed to do. She stood up and limped to the guest bedroom. She reached under the mattress and pulled out her journal. Sitting on the bed, she flipped through the pages. She had done so much work, and yet she had still failed. The feeling gnawed at her, disrupting her physiology and shooting her over the Stress Curve once again. She vaguely noticed she was growing more frustrated with each turn of the page. Finally, she closed the book and lay back on the bed.

Elizabeth, I need you, was the last thought she had before falling asleep, hoping for the best.

She woke to find herself standing on the Cozy Landing near the bookshelf, holding her journal. Elizabeth was across the room, looking out the window. She was surprised to see that Elizabeth was dressed in a tailored riding jacket with cream-colored breeches tucked into knee-high riding boots. Her hair was pulled back into a low, neat bun. Elizabeth turned around, and Ellie saw the ever-present black-rimmed glasses.

Ellie took a step toward her and felt the pain in her ankle. *Well, I guess magic only goes so far*, she half-smiled as she started to limp across the room.

Elizabeth turned around and smiled. "Oh my darling, I see you're limping," she said with warmth and concern. "That was a *nasty* fall."

Ellie made her way over and sat on the couch, followed by Elizabeth.

"I heard you call," Elizabeth began. "I would have come immediately, but I knew you needed to take some steps forward. I wondered whether you would come here or stay down there," she said, pointing casually to the door that led to the Basement of Shadows. Ellie felt her cheeks pinken as she understood the kind truth of Elizabeth's observations.

"You did so well!" Elizabeth proclaimed. "You took some deep breaths, got some sleep, pulled out your journal, and now, you're ready for the next part."

Ellie's forehead crinkled.

"You seem confused," Elizabeth said as their eyes met. "Tell me *everything*."

"I tried," Ellie said, forgetting to ask Elizabeth about the outfit she was wearing.

"You *tried* …" Elizabeth repeated kindly, urging her to continue.

Ellie went through it all. She shared about the victories she'd known and the momentum she had gained. Then she told the story about the tree root, raising her voice with Chase, and the argument with Joe. She was afraid that Chase had heard the things she had said.

"That had to be terribly discouraging," Elizabeth said kindly.

Ellie completed the story and finished with a deep sigh.

"Well, my dear, there's no other way to say it. Today was a setback. I'm so sorry."

There was a moment of silence.

Elizabeth continued, "Tell me more about the walk itself. Take me through it in *detail*."

"Well," Ellie replied, "I was feeling great until I tripped."

"There's something else," Elizabeth said. "Can you remember?"

Ellie sat and thought.

"What were you thinking about right before you tripped?"

"Oh," Ellie said, remembering. "I was thinking about Chase."

"Positive things?" Elizabeth asked.

"No. I was worried about him. And I was wondering if I can be the mom I need to be."

"And then you tripped?"

"Yup. Then I tripped."

"So, by the time you got back home, you must've been a mess," Elizabeth continued.

"Yeah. I wasn't in a good place."

"And then?" Elizabeth prodded.

"Chase tried to help, and I yelled at him. Then Joe told me that something else had happened at school. And then he started with the 'it's just a phase' stuff. And I let him have it."

They sat quietly for a few minutes. "Let me ask you this," Elizabeth said. "If this exact thing had happened to Grace, what would you say to her?"

Ellie thought again.

"First, I would tell her how sorry I was that all of this had happened to her."

"And then?" Elizabeth asked.

"Then, I would probably say that it wasn't the best time to get into it with her husband. I'd tell her since she wasn't in a good place, the conversation was bound to go wrong. She was hurt, surprised, and confused, and that's not a recipe for a successful talk with her husband."

"So, even though you were in the living room of your house, you were in …" Elizabeth said, letting the last words lead Ellie to the answer.

"The Basement of Shadows," she said.

"The Basement of Shadows," Elizabeth repeated. "How did that feel?"

"Kinda good and kinda bad," Ellie replied. "It felt good to let off steam and let Joe know how I felt. And it felt good to hurt him like he's hurt me. But afterward, I hated how distant I felt. And now, I've broken our connection pretty badly. I wish I hadn't done that."

"Did the way you acted help you move *toward* or *away* from the life you want to live?" Elizabeth asked.

"Of course, it was away," Ellie said despondently. Her ankle was throbbing. "What am I going to do?" she asked. "I didn't know it was going to be this hard."

Her *Victim Self* was rising, ready to take center stage. "I'm getting zero support from Joe. If only he would stop being so pigheaded about Chase, I might be able to make some progress," her *Blame-Shifting Self* added. "And I can't even get an appointment with someone who is supposedly the 'Best Pediatrician in the City.' And if I do, I know it's going to cost thousands of dollars we don't have. And I'm going to have to explain the whole thing from beginning to end before they can even start helping me. And who knows if they can even help me?" Ellie's voice was raised, and she was talking faster.

"Not to mention Chase's school," she continued. Her *Shadow Sisters* were coming out one by one. "They are so insensitive to his needs. The parents must all think I'm a lousy mom, and maybe I am. If they would just show a little consideration, I wouldn't be in this position. And Chase? Throwing sand at a little girl? What is going on with him?"

Ellie stopped and looked at Elizabeth. "I thought you promised that things would be different once I started working on myself," she defiantly finished, as if she were an attorney completing her closing argument.

"Lots of feelings," Elizabeth said after a moment, unresponsive to the emotions Ellie expressed. "I'm glad you got them out. They are real, and they have some real truth in them. And they all provide important information you could explore if you choose to. But first, let's start with the time leading up to today. You said you were doing well? Can you tell me more?"

"Nothing that did anything good, evidently," Ellie answered. "It feels like things are the same or even worse," she concluded.

"No. That will not do," Elizabeth said sternly. "Try again. What have you done right lately?"

Ellie was taken aback. Elizabeth had never used that tone of voice before. It was both startling and comforting.

Ellie thought through what she had done during the time leading up to the tree root incident. She shared about the times she had spent with Grace. She recounted the date she had set up with Joe to discuss working together on Chase's situation. She mentioned the appointment with the pediatrician. She talked about the walks that had started to become a part of her routine.

"I guess I did some things right," she finally said. "And *this* is where that got me," she said as she lifted her swollen ankle.

Elizabeth continued her firm tone. "This self-pity will not do," she began. "You can't just throw out all of the good things you've done because of this setback. I know you want things to be different," she concluded, "but it will take time. And there will be some twists and turns. That is to be expected. After all, it took a long time to get to this crisis; it's going to take some time to genuinely build your way out of it."

Ellie listened attentively.

"You see, my dearest," Elizabeth said, changing to a softer, more gentle tone. "To *do something* different, you have to *become someone* different. And that takes time. It's not a straight line. It's a part of growing. It's how you handle the failures that makes all the difference. And part of it is acknowledging the good things you have done along the way."

Elizabeth stood up and walked toward the bookcase. "If you only get to feel good when *everything* is right, you will have a long, sad life. But if you see that life is made up of victories and defeats, and you can celebrate the *progress* and take the time to pat yourself on the back along the way, your relationship with me, and therefore your HeartPrint, can become a part of your everyday life. So, let's start there," Elizabeth said, returning to the couch. "Open that beautiful journal of yours and write down your *accomplishments*."

Ellie took in the speech, sighed, and complied with her Wise Woman's request. Just opening the journal made Ellie feel better. She found one of the gold bookmark ribbons and opened to the page it marked. The page was blank. The pen pleasantly glided over the paper as it always did. She began to write down some of the good things she had done. As she wrote, she noticed she felt calmer. She felt a shift in her attitude.

When she finished, she looked up and saw Elizabeth at the bookshelf, touching some of the books there. Ellie sighed and said, "I see what you mean. That feels better. I guess those things were easy to forget."

"Well done, mon amie!" Elizabeth said as she walked across the Cozy Landing. "Please, make this a part of your daily life. The journal isn't just about working through your feelings. It's about commemorating your progress. It's about recording *your* journey to *your* HeartPrint."

They sat together quietly on the couch.

"That's a big part of it," Elizabeth said absentmindedly.

"A big part of what?" Ellie asked.

"I'm sorry," Elizabeth said, "I was lost in thought. A big part of growing is recognizing where we are emotionally *in the moment*.

"You see, we all have our patterns," she continued. "Maybe it starts with anxiety, like you worrying about Chase and being a good mother. Then, our faithful *Shadow Sisters* are more than willing to join in the conversation. Next comes blaming others for how we have been mistreated or misunderstood. Then, we lash out and break connections.

"It took a while for me to get that figured out," Elizabeth said. "You see, growth happens when you *know your patterns*, and you can identify when you are in one of them." Elizabeth was becoming animated. "It's something called *attunement*."

"Attunement," Ellie repeated.

"Let's take your walk as an example," Elizabeth said. "What if, when you recognized the anxiety you were feeling about yourself and Chase, you said out loud something as simple as 'I'm worried about Chase. It hurts to feel this way, and I wish it were different.' I wonder how everything would have turned out."

Ellie thought. "Well, people would think I was a crazy lady, talking to myself …"

They both laughed.

"But maybe it would have changed what happened after that," Ellie said reflectively.

"Yes," Elizabeth agreed. "I think if you had spoken your feelings out loud, it would have reminded you that thoughts like that are a warning sign. Maybe you wouldn't have gotten distracted."

"And maybe, I wouldn't have fallen." Ellie finished the thought. She was rubbing her knee. "I let my emotions get the best of me," she said.

"It's more like you didn't take the time to process them," Elizabeth replied, "because you weren't in attunement with them. Once you do that, you'll be amazed at how, well, profound the difference is."

Again, Ellie was quiet, thinking about what she had heard.

Elizabeth smiled. "Well, there are consequences to what happened today," she said, changing the subject. "You've broken your connection with Joe. You'll have to deal with that. And there's work to do with Chase. And I think you're on the right track." Looking at the journal, she said, "Let's come up with a plan—we always need a plan."

Ellie opened to the page that had her lists on it. She wrote:

Talk to Joe—the sooner the better
Have a talk with Chase about how I treated him
Follow up with the pediatrician
Get ready for the school meeting on Friday

Ellie looked at the list and thought about doing each of those things. "I don't think I know how to do all of this," she said.

Their eyes met. "Of course you don't know how to do it," Elizabeth said warmly. "If you knew how to do it, you wouldn't have these issues. We would be talking about something completely different!"

The words hung in the air.

"We can only work on what's *next for us*," she continued. "You will grow into a version of yourself that *can* do these things. Just think about how wonderful the next version of yourself will be. You will be closer to your HeartPrint. It's who you were meant to be."

Ellie sighed. She pictured herself being the kind of person who could handle each of these challenges. She closed her journal and stood up, wincing in pain. "I think I understand," she said softly, "I'll do my best."

Ellie began to write down some of the good things she had done.

From Elizabeth

I remember learning the word *attunement*. It was a very valuable find. I hope it will be helpful for you as well. When we are in an emotional crisis, we do not usually allow ourselves time to step back and process. If we could, we would avoid a lot of pain and confusion. If, for just a moment, we could give ourselves a bit of room for our Wise Woman to help us evaluate and process the situation in real time, it would make all the difference. Often, though, it's when we are building new skills that we need the most time to figure out a new way forward. Sometimes we need to take a break for longer in order to do the journal processing of knowing what we don't want, in order to figure out the plan to get to what we do want.

And that's not easy. It's natural to simply slip into our normal patterns and react from our emotions. We return to the older version of ourselves that continues to move us away from the life we want to live. Mainly because it's familiar and our brains feel safer with the known pathways. When we make this choice, like with Ellie, there are consequences.

You see, it takes a lot of energy and thoughtfulness to step back and give ourselves room *in the moment*. If we live a tired life most of the time, it's hard to find the strength to make any kind of change. If that's the case, we must find a way to bring more energy to our lives. Energy is an important part of connecting with your Wise Woman and your HeartPrint. It serves us well to take some time and consider the energy that surrounds our lives.

Every day, we can live in all kinds of different energies. First, there is low energy. This is what Ellie faced after her fall. When we are in that energy state, we make decisions that aren't connected to our HeartPrint. Even the simplest of tasks can seem overwhelming. Low energy and the Basement of Shadows go hand in hand. Have you ever felt like the idea of getting ready for the day just seemed like too much? That is low energy. Survival is the goal, not transformation.

Next, there is middle energy. It's not too high or too low. When we are in that energy state, we are productive and engaged with life. There are satisfying moments and disappointing events, but they all fall within a place where we can still regulate ourselves and decide what the next right thing is. It's actually a great place to live. It's real life. Your Wise Woman is leading you, and your HeartPrint is never far away.

Finally, there is high, positive energy. This brings those moments of profound gratitude, exhilaration, and unbridled joy. It's a time of celebration. These are precious moments—moments we experience while in the Beautiful Attic. From there, we have perspective and wonder.

None of us can live in the high-energy zone all the time because our bodies aren't made to live in this peak state. We all deserve moments in life when everything comes together like the flick of a switch. There will be days and even weeks like this as your Wise Woman leads you to your HeartPrint.

Let's dive a bit deeper. Here are some of the emotions that, if you are feeling them, are a part of the low-energy frame of mind.

Low Energy

- *Fatigued*—the idea of trying something different feels overwhelming because you just don't have the energy.
- *Feeling small*—believing you don't matter or that your voice carries no weight.
- *Disempowered*—sensing that life is happening *to* you, without choices or control.
- *Angry*—holding onto frustration that bursts out at others or quietly simmers inside. The more criticism and contempt you have, the bigger the box in the basement.
- *Unhappy*—experiencing a heaviness or sadness that lingers, no matter what you do.
- *Worthless*—thinking you have nothing to offer, or that others would be better off without you.

- **Self-critical**—hearing your inner voice that points out only flaws and mistakes.
- **Blaming others for problems**—shifting responsibility outward instead of pausing to see your own role.

These emotions are underneath the open browser tabs we have discussed. They must be recognized, externalized somehow, and processed. Otherwise, it's off to the Basement of Shadows for rumination.

Middle Energy

What about middle energy? As you can see in the list below, the emotions in this category are mostly positive. Yes, we might experience some of the low-energy emotions mentioned above (that's reality), but they don't dominate us. Instead, they are recognized, attuned to, and integrated.

- *Empowerment*—recognizing you can take meaningful action, even in small ways.
- *Warmth*—feeling an openness in your heart toward yourself and others.
- *Connection*—knowing you belong and that your relationships give life richness.
- *Satisfaction*—appreciating progress, even if everything isn't perfect.
- *Contentment*—resting in the present moment without craving more.
- *Strength*—trusting your resilience and ability to face what comes.
- *Grounded gratitude*—noticing the good things you already have—like family, health, and a safe place to rest—and letting them bring you peace.

Can you picture your life where those feelings are predominant? As you and your Wise Woman work together in your own special way, I'm happy to share with you that it's entirely possible.

High Energy

Finally, here are some of the emotions reserved for our Beautiful Attic:

- *Expansive*—sensing that your spirit is bigger than your circumstances; able to dream freely.
- *Joyous*—delighting in life with laughter, celebration, and playfulness.
- *Inspired*—feeling sparks of creativity and vision that seem to come from beyond yourself.
- *Boundlessness*—tasting freedom, as if no walls or ceilings can hold you back.
- *Overflowing gratitude*—overflowing thankfulness that lifts you higher, where even ordinary moments feel sacred.

High-energy emotions are precious when they come. Having the awareness that we are experiencing them makes them even more special.

Our energy does not live in a bubble. There are people and situations that affect it. Have you ever noticed some people raise your energy while others lower it? Maybe after you spend time with a certain friend, you always feel better. And maybe there's a relative who leaves you with low energy whenever you are around them. It's the same for situations. Some of them consistently give us medium energy, and some of them leave us only with low energy.

A good beginning is to start to recognize (attune to) what brings you energy and what drains your energy. Make note of the people and situations that arouse low-energy emotions. Recognize the people and situations that arouse middle- and high-energy emotions. Keep track of them in your journal. Make a plan to maximize the middle and high energy and be extra prepared when you know you will encounter low-energy situations and people.

I have one final thought before we move on to the next chapter. It's about patterns. Our brains *love* patterns and binary choices.

They like to keep it simple. If X happens, then Y must follow. Here's how it works: Our brain says, "When that happens, it means danger. You must protect yourself." Or, "When we hear that song, it means everything is alright."

For instance, if our brain sees someone who has brought us low energy many times before, it will instinctively go into protection mode whenever we see them. The secret is to attune to our body's wisdom and signals. When we do that, we can start to process the information that is coming in, allowing us to plan and make better decisions.

If you and your Wise Woman can attune to the information in the moment, you can make a Towards Move and choose a different decision than your pattern prescribes. Otherwise, you enter the familiar, largely unconscious, well-worn pattern that plays itself out, causing an unwelcome outcome.

Ellie had to learn the low-energy thought and behavior pattern that started when she thought about Chase's future. She had to recognize this pattern would inevitably lead to a state of worry, anxiety, and frustration, and her *Shadow Sisters* were close by to join in the conversation.

When she was out walking and tripped over that root, she reached a decision point. Would she repeat the same old thinking, or would she choose something different? In that moment, the only path forward she could see was the one that was well-worn. As she limped back to the house, her *Shadow Sisters* of defensiveness and blame-shifting joined her in the Basement of Shadows. This led to the fight with Joe. She broke the connection between herself, Joe, and Chase, and lost the positive momentum she had built. Once the *Shadow Sisters* had gone, she was left to face the uncomfortable consequences of her human fallibility moment.

I like to lighten this topic and call this process the Chicken Dance. Do you remember the dance? It's kind of a polka song. When the music comes on, you mimic the actions of a chicken. First, you make a beak with your arms, then you flap your "wings." Next, you put your hands behind you and imitate tail feathers. You end the pattern by clapping your hands four times. The funny part of it is that as the music gets faster and faster, you have to repeat the pattern more quickly. Our emotional Chicken Dance is when we go through these unconscious, repetitive patterns that lead us inevitably to the Basement of Shadows.

It is part of being human. Our patterns are well rehearsed and almost always unconscious. Have you ever daydreamed while driving your car? You arrive somewhere but don't really remember the journey. That is our beautiful brain running the show while we are distracted. That same thing can happen with low energy, *Shadow Sisters*, and the Basement of Shadows. We find ourselves there without even being aware of how we got there.

For Ellie, her Chicken Dance was to start with worry, move to distraction, continue to helplessness, and finish with withdrawal and anger. Whenever she did that dance as a way to protect herself from her feelings, she moved away from me and her HeartPrint. She didn't know how to do anything different. It was a very difficult thing for her to notice and then choose to change.

Ellie's Chicken Dance (What's Yours?)

Finally, most of all, I want you to understand the journey of living in coherence with your Wise Woman and your HeartPrint is never a straight line. There will be steps forward and steps backward. Across your lifetime, you will explore, try, fail, succeed, and grow. You will notice that whenever you live in your HeartPrint, your internal world will be attuned, and you will take inspired action toward your life, dreams, and goals. Your external world will start to match your internal one. That, my friend, is a wonderful way to live your life, and it's where true contentment and satisfaction come from.

Speaking of growing, the next story was a profound turning point in Ellie's life. And the source of wisdom came from a young woman called Miss Keene.

A Cup of Tea with Meg

This chapter is about energy, patterns, and attunement. I have one question for each of these:

- Can you make a list of what brings you low, medium, and high energy? Take some time to write these things down.
- Can you identify a conscious or unconscious pattern you follow that leads you away from your Wise Woman and your HeartPrint?
- How easy or hard is it for you to attune to your feelings in the moment and take a step back to allow yourself to respond differently to the situation?
- How often do you reflect on things that don't go well, and find new Towards Moves that allow you to do them differently the next time?

Chapter 12 · Age 43

Maple Grove Elementary, principal's office with Miss Keene—a difficult moment of recognition

Ellie awoke from her midday recovery-from-her-big-feelings nap with her journal next to her. She quietly slipped it under the mattress and stood up. She limped down the hall and into the kitchen, where Joe was fixing lunch. When she came into the room, he asked, "How are you feeling?"

Joe and Ellie had a pattern where, after a fight, they would both be extra nice to each other. Sometimes they wouldn't talk about the fight at all. Other times, the fight would reignite. Ellie was determined to handle this conversation differently.

"I'm feeling better, thank you for asking ... Also, I'd like to talk about what happened this morning and the things I said," she began sincerely. "But I'm just not ready to do it now. I need some more time to get it together, and I don't want us to fight again. I'm sorry for the way things went."

"Okay ..." Joe said tentatively. He wasn't used to talks going this way. "Do you need to go to the doctor?" he asked.

"I don't think so," Ellie replied. "I think I just need some time. I don't think I'm up for dinner tonight."

"Sure," Joe said. "I was going to run some errands," he continued. "But I can stay here and help if you need me to."

"No, go ahead," Ellie said. "I'll be fine."

Joe left with his sandwich. Ellie sat down on a chair, contemplating her most recent visit with Elizabeth.

The rest of the day passed without incident. That night, Ellie had a vivid dream. She and Joe were at the beach with Chase. She felt the warm sun on her face and watched the cool ocean breeze flapping a towel lying on the sand. Chase was playing in the sand, and Joe was asleep on the lounge chair next to her. The sound of the seagulls and the crashing waves comforted her. She caught a glimpse of someone walking along the beach who looked like Elizabeth. She felt the warmth of contentment move through her bones.

Over the next few days, Ellie's ankle began to improve. Even though she couldn't go on her walks, she faithfully journaled most days. She initiated a conversation with Joe, where they discussed the details of what had happened on the day she'd tripped. It was much easier to discuss things without the emotions of the moment. They came up with a new plan for the next time they faced something similar. Ellie would let Joe know she was feeling overwhelmed, and Joe would give her a couple of hours to regain her balance. Then, they would come back together, and Joe would find out what he could do to support her.

Just that conversation seemed to change their dynamic. Joe seemed more attentive and positive. Ellie thought maybe the change in him mirrored her commitment to handling their disagreements differently.

She also sat down and had a talk with Chase about what had happened when she'd tripped. To her relief, she discovered he hadn't heard the things she'd said to Joe about him. Ellie sincerely apologized to her son. She knew there was more healing work to do there, and the talk was a step in the right direction.

Ellie researched possible alternative schools for Chase. She was productive and pleasant at work. Things were getting back on track.

Her *Shadow Sisters* would speak to her from time to time. They let her know that low energy was nearby, and they offered her their version of care and concern. She would take their feedback into consideration, but not react. She was better attuned to her feelings. More than once, she quietly spoke out loud about what she was currently feeling. Once they were spoken, she was mostly able to process them, so her *Shadow Sisters* didn't take center stage.

As she continued to focus on her internal growth, she started noticing little moments of the day that made her appreciative, like when Chase genuinely thanked her for making his favorite sandwich after school. It was a good few days.

On Thursday morning, Joe was running late for work and couldn't find his keys. He became animated and angry. Ellie noticed she was starting to mirror Joe's emotions. She felt her stress begin to rise.

"When he gets angry, I get anxious," she said out loud to herself.

She thought about it and decided it didn't have to happen that way. *Let me try to be supportive*, she thought.

She walked into the kitchen and said, "Losing keys can be so frustrating. Let me help."

She started looking around for the keys. Joe's voice was raised as he searched, recounting that "Someone must have put them somewhere." Ellie again resisted the urge to react.

"They're here somewhere," she said patiently.

A few minutes later, Joe found the keys in his jacket pocket. "I don't know how they got there," he said sheepishly. "Thanks for helping."

He hurried out the door. Ellie stood still for a moment and appreciated her growth. *Something for the "Things to Notice and Appreciate" part of my journal*, she thought as she returned to packing her lunch for work.

Friday morning came—the day they were scheduled to meet with the principal at Chase's school to discuss the issues in the classroom and playground. As the two of them drove to the school, Ellie's *Shadow Sisters* filled her mind with critical, blame-shifting thoughts.

"I don't like Principal Haynes," Ellie said nervously and defensively. "I don't think he really cares about Chase."

Joe grunted. "But I liked Miss Keene when we met her at the beginning of the year," he said, referring to Chase's teacher. "And maybe we need to give Principal Haynes a chance."

Ellie felt defensive. Her *Angry Self* felt the urge to get into an argument. Instead, she stopped herself. Maybe Joe was just trying to be helpful. Maybe, she thought, getting into an argument with him as they were driving to the appointment was not the best idea. Ellie took a deep breath. "Maybe …" she said. "I'll guess we'll see."

They walked through the school hall and into the office where Principal Haynes and Miss Keene were waiting. There were four chairs arranged around a coffee table across the room from the principal's desk.

"Please, have a seat," Principal Haynes said, gesturing to the chairs. After Ellie and Joe declined a cup of coffee, the conversation began.

"We're here today to discuss ways we can help Chase," the principal began. "It's been a few weeks since school started, and there have been a few instances where we've seen him struggle. Although we are concerned this has been disruptive to his classmates, the larger discussion is what we all can do together to understand and support Chase."

Ellie was surprised. She had a whole conversation in her mind about how this was going to go. Principal Haynes would subtly accuse them of being bad parents. She would defend herself and Chase (but not Joe). She even had her final statement ready: "Well, maybe it's time for us to look at different schools." She pictured herself raising her voice, pointing her finger, and storming out of the office. Her *Shadow Sisters* weren't far away. Her *Defensive Self* engaged, attempting to protect her from feeling vulnerable about needing support for her parenting and potentially getting hurt. She did not expect anything resembling a supportive conversation.

"We'd like to begin by having you, his parents, share your thoughts."

Ellie was quiet, taking in this unexpected change of tone. Joe spoke. Ellie tried to listen as he talked about Chase being a good kid and this was just a phase he was going through. She noticed both Principal Haynes and Miss Keene listened attentively. *Can they actually be buying what he's saying?* whispered her *Contemptuous Self*.

After Joe had finished, Principal Haynes asked, "And what about you, Mrs. Rhodes? What are your thoughts?"

Ellie's *Defensive Self* wasn't buying into it. It was probably a good cop, bad cop thing. She started the speech she had prepared earlier.

"Look, we are just trying to find a way to help Chase," she said tersely. "We know he isn't acting appropriately. We don't like his behavior any more than you do. We have tried talking with him and punishing him. We want this behavior to stop." She felt a flush of embarrassment for speaking so coldly about her son.

"Thank you," Principal Haynes said gently, without further comment. "Miss Keene," he said, looking at Chase's teacher, "what do you see in the classroom?"

Miss Keene, a young woman with reddish, shoulder-length hair, sat up straight and scooched to the front of her chair. She smiled. "Well, first of all, I think Chase is a terrific kid."

Yeah, sure, Ellie's *Angry Self* said to her. *This is a setup. She's going to say something nice and then let Chase have it. Here comes the "but."*

"And," she surprisingly continued, "I think if we all work together, we can figure this out." She sat back in her chair, not offering anything more.

There was a moment of silence. Ellie quickly searched her mind to make sense of the situation. How was this going to play out? Was Principal Haynes going to drop the other shoe?

"Please, Miss Keene, continue," Principal Haynes finally said.

Staying seated back in the chair, Miss Keene said, "Well, I've noticed a few things about when Chase is having a hard time and is overwhelmed. There seem to be some patterns."

The word *patterns* grabbed Ellie's attention, since she and Elizabeth had just discussed them in their last talk. Now it was Ellie's turn to sit up straight and edge to the front of her chair. She listened carefully.

"I was curious about his struggles. I noticed Chase is generally a balanced kid. He interacts well with his classmates most of the time. Until he doesn't. This told me that Chase is capable of healthy interactions. So there must be something that triggers him to act out. Have you noticed anything like this at home?" she asked, looking at Ellie.

Ellie was trying to process this new information and reorient herself. She had come into the meeting ready to defend and oppose. She noticed her breath was high in her chest, and consciously practiced belly breathing to regulate herself.

Joe noticed she needed some extra time and spoke first. "Well, like I said, he's a good kid at home most of the time. Then he'll have these weird outbursts. I usually just send him to his room until he gets over it."

Ellie still couldn't find any words. She was breathing from her belly and trusting her Wise Woman would come back online soon.

Miss Keene continued. "I think there's an opportunity here for us to support and accommodate Chase. Mrs. Rhodes, have you noticed anything at home that might help provide an environment that really works for him?"

Ellie searched her mind for what to say next. Finally, she decided just to be honest. "I've never thought about that," she said somewhat defeatedly.

"Well," Miss Keene said, "let's think about it together. The sand-throwing incident happened at recess after lunch last Tuesday. Do you remember anything unusual about that day?"

Ellie thought back. "Last Tuesday? Yes, I remember we were in a hurry that morning, and I didn't have time to fix him lunch, so I just gave him a turkey sandwich and a bruised banana. He doesn't like either of them. He came back with both of them in the bag."

"That's interesting," Miss Keene said. "And another outburst happened right after we completed a pretty tough project in class. Maybe those are some clues."

"I remember one time he kicked a chair at home," Joe chimed in. "It was right after I had him clean up a mess he'd made on the floor. I thought he was just mad about it. I sent him to his room."

"I've noticed Chase can be pretty intense," Miss Keene said. "He really pours himself into his work. Maybe these outbursts happen when he's hungry or drained from working so hard."

Ellie thought back to other times Chase had acted out. For the first time, she began to see the pattern. She remembered times when he'd skipped breakfast. She pictured how intensely he worked on a project. How could she have missed this?

Miss Keene continued. "Maybe a good plan is for you to pack something like an extra protein bar, if he likes them, every day as a backup. And I'll try to make sure he has some quiet time between activities to let himself reset. You could try that at home as well."

Ellie nodded quietly.

After a few seconds of silence, Principal Haynes spoke up. "Thank you, Miss Keene," he said, indicating the meeting was coming to an end. "Let's give this a shot and see if it makes a difference." He stood up. "Thanks for coming in today," he said. "This is a team effort."

They all stood up and started walking toward the door. Ellie stopped, turned around, and walked toward Miss Keene, who was walking behind them. She couldn't leave without saying something.

"I'm not sure what to say," she started. Her voice quivered. "But thank you. Thank you for ..." her mind couldn't find the words. "Thank you for *seeing* our son," she finally said.

Miss Keene smiled and said, "Of course! He really is a great kid. We will figure this out together."

Ellie was quiet on the ride home and for the rest of the day. Joe tried to discuss the meeting, but Ellie could only give grunts and vague answers. That night, after Joe and Chase had gone to bed, Ellie opened her journal and began to write.

It started with her writing down all of her big feelings. She began with, "Am I a bad mother?" across the top of the page. She scribbled on one side of the journal her feelings for Chase, both positive and negative. On the other side, she wrote out things she had done and was doing for him. Then she wrote, "Why did I not see him?" underlining the word "see." She listed out some possible reasons.

Then, she simply wrote, "Elizabeth ..." She sat and contemplated all she had written, trying to process her feelings in a new way. After a few minutes, she ended her evening with this:

Lesson today: too focused on everything Chase wasn't doing and I let that define our relationship.

Forgot to see how wonderful he can be ...

Need to see him as a person, not just what he does.

I expect him to disappoint me.

He must pick that up from me.

She continued to explore her feelings. She wrote:

Chase =

> *Sensitive*
> *Smart*
> *Cares about doing things right*
> *Very intense*

He needs more support—my fault.

I blame myself.

I see myself in him when I get frustrated with Joe ...

She continued to write:

Chase's triggers:

> *Hunger*
> *Things that are hard for him*

Chapter 12 • Age 43

I feel like a bad mom.

I want to be a good mom.

What can I do to move things in the right direction?

> *Should I talk to him about this?*
> *Do I need professional help?*
> *Healthy lunches (make sure he likes them)*
> *Quiet times after hard things*
> *Attune to my frustrations with him*

Ellie closed her journal with a deep, reflective sigh. She reread the words she had written, each line a step toward a greater understanding. The *Shadow Sisters* were *finally* silent, and she was no longer in the Basement of Shadows with this situation.

Ellie had processed her feelings, learned from them, and gained a new perspective. It was good to be on the Cozy Landing, working through things without Elizabeth there. She realized this avoidance of working through her feelings had been a long-standing issue for her, starting from her childhood. Now, through Chase and Joe, she was learning to handle her confusion differently from what she had been shown as a child.

As she sat in the quiet, memories surfaced—moments when she could have been a better guide to her son; times when her actions had unknowingly added to his struggles. Then, her mind recounted the way her father and mother had treated her. She wasn't blaming them, but it helped her understand. She could see how she had a tendency to parent Chase the same way she had been parented. That connection allowed her to start to make changes in the intergenerational pattern. She was immensely comforted and encouraged, but also very sad about how all of this had impacted Chase.

She acknowledged her guilt, shame, and fear about what she might have done to damage her son. She also noticed she had hope. There was a sense of purpose and a cautious excitement for the possibilities ahead. Tomorrow wasn't just another day; it was a chance to begin again with her son.

"Thank you for seeing our son."

From Elizabeth

I tear up almost every time I remember this day. Ellie, for the first time, understood that her issues were becoming Chase's issues. It was heartbreaking. It was also a pivotal moment for her.

As you may have noticed, I was nowhere to be found in this story. Miss Keene stood in for me and did a great job. I have discovered that wisdom can come from any number of places. Maybe it's a person like a teacher, pastor, parent, or friend. It could come to you by reading a book, listening to a podcast, or watching a particular scene in a movie or TV show. It can sometimes be found by speaking with a professional. Once we become aware of our *need for wisdom*, it makes itself known in all sorts of unexpected places.

I'm reminded here of how deeply our lives are shaped by the generations before us. We, in turn, shape the lives that follow ours. If you have children, no matter their age, I hope you can see them not just as your kids, but as fellow travelers. Like us, they are trying to find their way. Like us, they need understanding, guidance, and support.

Allow me to share a quote from Sigmund Freud. I don't agree with everything he said, but I love this:

"Love and work, work and love ... that's all there is."

My hope for you is that you will discover the simple joy of living each day fully. That you will embrace the challenges each day brings. I hope you will find a type of "work" or community contribution you can make, and in doing so, bring purpose to your life—a life where you nurture your relationships and show up as the best version of yourself. A life where you practice loving—loving yourself, and loving your people. Work is love. And love is work.

Ellie was living that way before the meeting. She was making small changes, like choosing a different response when Joe lost his keys. In fact, they weren't really small at all. In the simple act of reacting differently when Joe was getting stressed out, she changed the *feeling* in her home and herself, at least for a few moments. As women, I think we are often the cultural tone-setters in the home. I believe we have much more influence than we realize or allow ourselves to notice.

Have you ever thought about the fact that it only takes one person to change a dynamic? When we change how we bring ourselves into a situation, it changes the *situation*. We do not *have to* do our well-worn Chicken Dance. We can choose a different response and make a Toward Move that changes the dynamic.

When our Loved Ones perform their Chicken Dances, we do not have to join in. We can respond from our Cozy Landing selves. Remember that it's not about perfection. We don't have to get it 100 percent right every time. We can work toward responding from our Wise Woman space 80 percent of the time. This gives us room for our very human selves. As Ellie changed, the atmosphere in her home changed. Her marriage benefited, and she and Joe grew closer over time. Small changes often lead to bigger victories eventually.

There will be setbacks. We saw this happen in the car on the way to the meeting. The battle began again. Ellie was triggered by the psychological threat to her son's well-being (if this meeting didn't go well). In the midst of her trepidation, her *Shadow Sisters* appeared on center stage to make their case as a way to protect her. She felt an onslaught of low-energy emotions. She tried her best, but she was definitely in a defensive mindset as she went into the meeting. She was braced for a confrontation. She had already played it out (and thereby ruminated over it) in her mind countless times.

This was truly a pivotal point for Ellie. Both in the car and in the principal's office, she worked to remain open to new information and a new perspective, despite the feedback from her *Shadow Sisters*. Ellie resisted the temptation to let this situation play out as she had imagined it. Choosing to think and act differently directly changed the course of her life, and Chase's, too. Indirectly, it also brought her closer to Joe. It truly was a breakthrough moment.

Looking back on it, there were four steps that allowed Ellie to handle this difficult situation differently:

1. **She attuned herself**—She created space between her and her emotions and acknowledged them without judgment.
2. **She had a perspective shift**—She paused and allowed the information from her attuned self to weigh a different perspective.
3. **She decided**—She didn't use the immediate emotions that arose to make her decision; she breathed until she settled, and then made a decision that came from her Wise Woman.
4. **She acted**—She took concrete steps based on the decision she'd made.

It's one thing for her to see the words on a page. But translating all of that into action took a lot of *energy*. Moving toward our Heart-Print is not an easy thing, especially at first. But if we can find the energy to make that move, the payoff is totally worth it. With each "box in the basement" that gets resolved, we have more energy for the next issue. Eventually, it is possible to experience life in a brand-new way. It can transform how we feel about ourselves, our relationships, and our happiness. Yes, it can be a long-term process, and that's okay. It takes however long it takes. At the end, we genuinely and congruently build our way out toward a life that feels good.

What I really love about Miss Keene is how she was curious, not judgmental, about Chase's behavior. Ellie was so connected emotionally to her son's actions that she wasn't able to take a step back and see them in context. Ellie needed the 10,000-foot view Miss Keene had. Miss Keene was someone with some experience, distance, and perspective. This is where community can be so very beneficial.

In contrast, Ellie had seen Chase's behavior at times as irritating, embarrassing, and troubling. She stopped there, mired in low-energy emotions and the *Shadow Sisters*' constant commentary. She played it all out in the Chicken Dance of emotions and reactions. Ellie couldn't get past her circular thinking to the point of becoming curious and exploring *why* Chase had acted the way he did. She couldn't see the connection between the way she had been parented and the way she was parenting. She had been wrapped up in herself, not *seeing* her child. Miss Keene had given her another way to view the situation.

After that meeting, Ellie started asking questions like:

- What stressful things lead Chase to these outbursts?
- Which of his needs are going unmet?
- What skills does he need to develop to deal with his stress?

Ellie began to see Chase as an actual person, not as a problem to fix. He was another human who was simply missing a piece of the puzzle. Rather than labeling him as "an angry child" or as one who was "just looking for attention," she shifted her focus to what was standing in his way and what he needed to build.

She stopped seeing him as willful or defiant and began to understand his struggles weren't about disobedience; they were about him not having the skills to handle situations when he was overwhelmed. She realized it wasn't a matter of rewards and punishment, but about things Chase *could not yet handle*. With that insight, Ellie started building the support her son truly needed.

So, it turns out that Ellie started to apply the same things she was learning about herself to her son. And that changed everything. Big changes began to happen. Ellie's relationship with Chase began to transform. The atmosphere at home continued to improve. Joe and Ellie talked more and continued to work through their issues. Ellie moved steadily toward a stronger connection to me and her HeartPrint.

The next story is one of my favorites. I hope you like it.

A Cup of Tea with Meg

This part explores things like finding wisdom from outside ourselves and being curious about behaviors and feelings instead of being judgmental. It also gives us a simple framework for working through our big feelings. Here are some questions I hope are helpful:

- Where have you found wisdom in unexpected places? Who are these special people? What did they teach you?
- When was the last time you were able to set aside your *Shadow Sisters* and bring your *Curious Self* to the discussion?
- How helpful is the Attune, Perspective Shift, Decide, and Act framework for you? Where is one place you could use it this week?

Chapter 13 · Age 44

the Ansonia Animal Shelter where Hugo lived—time in the Beautiful Attic

"Mom, are we really going to see Hugo this weekend?"

Chase was sitting at the counter, eating breakfast on a Thursday morning, a couple of months after the meeting with Miss Keene. There had been no more major incidents at school and only a few minor skirmishes at home. The family was in a good, positive flow. Ellie's ankle had healed, and she was back to taking walks most days. She was following the plan, and her days were filled with more hope and ease than before. She was growing steadily more in tune with her HeartPrint. Her attunement wasn't perfect (that wasn't her goal) but it was real. She had kept her *Shadow Sisters* from taking center stage. She was noticing more and more when they were activated. She was able to mostly listen to what they were worried about. There voices were much more about gathering information now, and so there was far less Chicken-Dancing drama.

"Yes!" Ellie said as she refilled Chase's orange juice. "There will be Hugo, camping, and lots of eating."

"I love Hugo," Chase said plainly.

"I think tortoises are kind of hard to love," Ellie replied. "But I'm glad you get to see him."

"Mom," Chase said, smiling earnestly, "I think they are *easy* to love."

Ellie noticed Chase's dream for her to love what he loved, so she took a breath and attuned to him. "You know what, honey, you're right," she said. "Tortoises are very wise and beautiful."

Chase's shoulders dropped in almost imperceptible relief, and he flashed a small smile of satisfaction. *Another entry into the appreciation page*, Ellie thought to herself as she smiled.

Chase and Ellie had "adopted" Hugo the tortoise at the Ansonia Animal Shelter, about a two-hour drive away from their home. Ellie knew Chase loved going there, and she was excited to share a weekend with him. Chase was as contented and open as Ellie could remember.

Ellie said, "It's time for school. Tomorrow afternoon, we ride!" Ellie tossed Chase's backpack onto the counter after checking to make sure the protein bar was included. "We ride!" Chase repeated, grabbing the backpack and sprinting to the garage.

The next day, Ellie packed the car and picked up Chase early from school, and they headed out of town. They sang along with the music from their special playlist, stopped for an ice cream, and finally arrived at the sanctuary around 4:00 p.m. They met with the young guide and were directed to their campsite, where the tent that was provided lay on the ground, ready to be erected.

"Do you need some help with the tent?" the guide asked. His badge revealed his name as Bob. He was a young man but adept at working with kids.

"Nope. We got this," Ellie replied. "Don't we, Chase?"

"When do I get to see Hugo?" Chase replied.

"Yes," Ellie said in mock seriousness to Bob, "When *do* we get to see Hugo?"

"I think he will be there for dinner," Bob replied, winking at Ellie and giving Chase a wry smile. "But only if the tent is set up."

Chase ran over to the tent and began lifting it off the ground. "Let's do this!" he shouted.

After thanking Bob, Ellie went over to the tent. "Do you think we can handle this?" Ellie asked him.

"Simple," Chase replied. "These poles go here," he said as he lifted one of them off the ground. "Then the tent goes on top," he continued. "And we hammer those things into the ground," he happily concluded, pointing to the tent stakes.

Before Ellie could respond, Chase was hard at work. She felt the urge to tell him to slow down and let her lead, but decided to let him do his work. She recognized this was a part of his HeartPrint.

"Do you want my help?" she asked.

"I've got this, Mom," Chase replied, connecting poles and trying them out on different parts of the tent.

Ellie sat down at the picnic table nearby, soaking in the moment.

She watched as Chase tried repeatedly to lift the tent into place, but each time it fell back to the ground, whooshing air.

"This stupid pole won't go where it's supposed to," Chase finally said.

He kicked the tent in frustration.

Ellie thought for a moment.

"I'll tell you what," she said. "Why don't you come over here and sit next to me for a minute? Let's think about it. Besides, I want to hear more about Hugo."

Chase threw a pole on the ground. "This tent is stupid!" he said.

"Come here," Ellie said gently, patting the seat next to her. "Let's talk about it."

Chase stomped over and sat down next to her.

"You're really smart," she said softly into his ear and reached into her purse for his favorite snack, a peanut butter granola bar. "We'll figure it out. First, eat this snack and tell me everything you like about Hugo."

Chase took a deep breath, opened the granola bar, and had a bite. His attention turned to Hugo. He began describing the things he liked about the giant tortoise. "Well," he said, "He's big—really big. And funny."

"Funny?" Ellie asked.

"Yeah, it's like he's an old man. He's wrinkly and quiet. He's never in a hurry."

Ellie sighed. "Yup. I like that about him, too. What else?"

As Chase talked more about Hugo and the energy from the protein bar balanced the work of putting the tent together, Ellie could sense his distress leaving. After a few minutes, she said, "Well, I can't wait for us to see him. But Bob the Guide said the tent must go up first. Let's work on it together."

They rose from the table and walked over to the tent. Ellie still let Chase take the lead, but she helped him out when she was needed. A few minutes later, the tent was assembled, their cots were set up, and the car was unpacked.

Ellie looked at her watch. "Guess what?" she said. "Turtle time?"

"You mean tortoise time, Mom. We've discussed this …"

Ellie laughed. "That's right. I forgot how much you know about turtles … I mean tortoises … which are definitely *not* terrapins!"

They walked together to the main camp, where Hugo and the other animals were waiting. Chase ran over and sat on the ground next to Hugo. He petted the tortoise and spoke to him in a low voice while offering him some lettuce to eat. Ellie sat a nearby picnic table. She was touched by her son's affection for the animal.

Chase eventually came and sat next to her.

"How's Hugo?" she asked.

"He's having a tough day," Chase replied.

"How so?"

"He said he gets stressed out in places like this, with all the people around. It kinda makes him mad."

Ellie saw her opportunity. "I get it. I get that way sometimes …" she said.

Chase sat quietly. "Yeah, me too," he said.

"I wonder how we could help Hugo," Ellie replied.

"Maybe he needs some more food. I think he gets hangry," Chase declared.

"Hangry? Where did you learn that word?" Ellie asked.

"Miss Keene told me about it. She said the cure is a protein bar," he concluded.

"That Miss Keene. I like her," Ellie said.

"Yeah, she's nice. Can we go see the llamas?" he asked, forgetting about Hugo for the moment.

"Yup. Let's go see the llamas. Have you named *them* yet?" Ellie asked as they walked toward the pair of animals.

"That one looks like Michael Jackson," Chase said, laughing.

Ellie laughed too.

"And that one's name is … I don't know, what do you think, Mom?"

"Oh, I don't know," Ellie said. "How about Beatrice?"

"Beatrice?" Chase giggled.

Ellie picked up her long, gangly son, noticing the effort it took. It wouldn't be long before he would be too big to lift. It was a bittersweet reminder of how life changes.

The rest of the camping trip was magical. They went on walks, ate campfire meals, and made new friends. Ellie began to see who Chase might become as a young man. A lot of the time during the weekend, she wasn't his mom; they were just kindred spirits enjoying each other's company. That part was deeply rewarding for Ellie. She took in how industrious he was. She saw his compassion and love for nature. Her fondness and appreciation for him grew as she saw him moving ever closer to his own unique HeartPrint.

Sunday afternoon came around, and it was time to leave. On the drive home, Chase fell asleep. Ellie had a moment of absolute clarity. She knew who she was and what she was here to do. She was filled with gratitude for her life. She noticed Chase rubbing his nose as he slept. She appreciated the sun as it was setting over the woods to the side of the highway. She felt relaxed, rejuvenated, and energized.

Her eyes welled up with tears as she noticed the affection she felt toward her son. She quietly thanked God, or the Universe (she wasn't sure), for Chase and for Miss Keene. She was fully present, in the moment. Ellie smiled as she thought about Elizabeth, who was becoming more and more a part of who she was. A transcendent clarity opened in her, and Ellie finally understood what Elizabeth meant by the Beautiful Attic. Her HeartPrint was shining brightly, and she was sure she could hear Elizabeth telling her she was proud of her.

Ellie sat a nearby picnic table. She was touched by her son's affection for the animal.

From Elizabeth

What a wonderful memory this trip is! It was a special time when Ellie visited the Beautiful Attic. She had been growing toward the life she wanted to live. I was so proud of her as she helped Chase through a hard moment. They formed a bond on the trip that continued to bloom long after the trip ended.

Once again, I am notable in my absence in this story. Ellie and I were working together each day, in regular conversation through her journal and internal thoughts. We had a channel open where we could talk directly by now, but no additional support was needed here. Ellie and I conversed as she chose different ways to connect with Chase, reflect on each of their unique HeartPrints, and attune with her Wise Woman during the trip. She was becoming competent in her growth and able to stand on her own. Ellie had located me and her HeartPrint and was living in it most of the time.

Which brings up the question, How's it going with your Wise Woman? Do you spend regular time with her? You know, they say it takes over 100 hours of time spent together to develop a close friendship.

Is your Wise Woman helping you by asking good questions? Remember, your Wise Woman will be different from me, but the same. She's that part of you who doesn't react in the moment but puts some space between the stimulus and the response. She always listens without judgment. She helps you to ask good questions and to come up with a plan to deal with whatever stress or challenges you face, together. She's a good friend who wants nothing but the best for you.

This brings us to the end of the Second Part of the book. I hope it's been a good journey for you. With your permission, I'd like to close out this part by going through some of the lessons Ellie and I learned along the way. May they be helpful reminders on the path to your HeartPrint.

Lesson 1: Our Pain Is Our Guide

Whenever we feel emotional pain, it's like a compass pointing us to where our next work is to be done. Try not to avoid, push away, or hate the pain. I invite you to partner with it, like you're slinging your Wise Woman arm around it. Then curiously and kindly ask the pain what it wants you to know and allow it to be the teacher it is.

Lesson 2: Attunement

Becoming aware of what we are feeling in the moment and being able to separate ourselves from that feeling, even for a brief moment, gives us space to create room for a choice point, which always allows us access to a sense of personal agency to handle the situation differently than we have before.

Lesson 3: We Are Made Up of Many Parts

We have called them the *Shadow Sisters*. They can be immature and childish. They might be defensive, critical, aggressive, argumentative, manipulative, or pouty. They each make us who we are. The tendency is to revile them, but that isn't helpful. It's important to remember they want to help and protect us. They just need to understand that although their voices are heard, they are not taking center Stage; our Wise Woman is. We also have plenty of positive parts that we haven't spent time on here, but they are in all of us.

Lesson 4: Towards and Away Moves

Every day, we have countless decisions to make about how we react to people and situations. Each of those reactions either moves us toward our HeartPrint or away from it. This simple knowledge can be life-changing.

Lesson 5: The Stories We Tell Ourselves

We all have a narrative of why we behave the way we do. A lot of these stories were formed when we were younger. They shape how we view ourselves, others, and the world. If we can identify our stories and look at them objectively, and process the pain and confusion behind them, we can heal and grow.

Our beautiful brains need to make sense of our lives and relationships. When our brain doesn't have all the information, it feels threatened, and offers suggestions to fill in the gaps of what is happening to us. We often create stories that are actually only partially true, and hold on to them for a long time as absolute truth. These stories can harm us because they are incomplete. We can heal the pain behind the stories, which truthfully and healthily can change the stories we tell ourselves. This gives us a clearer path to our Wise Woman and our HeartPrint.

Lesson 6: Energy

We can't grow without having sufficient physical and emotional energy. Think of it as bandwidth. Maybe the best thing we can do is start there. How can you add more energy to your life? Where can you carve out time for things that nourish and energize you? Without energy, it's very difficult (but not impossible) to build a life that allows you to gain the energy for the work ahead.

Lesson 7: The Stress Curve

We are always somewhere on the Stress Curve. Recognizing where we are can help us make decisions in the moment. We can build our life so we spend as much time as possible in the state of flow. That's the place where our bodies feel physiologically balanced, and we feel like we are in a space where we are able to manage what's on our plate, with a little bit of stretch. This is where humans thrive. You will always need to prioritize rest after being "in the zone," even when the work is good for you.

Lesson 8: Externalize

Something amazing happens when we take what is going on inside of us and externalize it. Maybe it's talking to a trusted friend. Or maybe it's setting a time with a professional therapist. It could be as simple as writing in your journal, or speaking out loud while looking in the mirror, or recording your feelings on your phone. If we can honestly externalize our true feelings and thoughts without the fear of judgment, and without invoking our *Shadow Sisters* to take center stage, which leads us to the Basement of Shadows, we are well on our way to a life that feels good. When we add some processing and curious questioning with empathy and validation for our struggles, we are really moving.

I hope these thoughts will serve you along your journey. Well, that's it for the first two parts. If you've made it this far, it means you are serious about discovering your HeartPrint and drawing ever closer to your Wise Woman. That encourages me immensely. Following a brief interlude, we are ready to return for the rest of the story. Ellie's life is full of twists, turns, joys, and sorrows. Let the adventure continue!

A Cup of Tea with Meg

As we conclude the Second Part of the book, it might be a good time to reflect on the lessons Elizabeth just shared.

Go through each of them and think about:

- Which ones make the most sense to you?
- Which ones do you want to focus on as your next Towards Move so you can live more often in your HeartPrint?

Give yourself the gift of not just skimming through these; instead, open your journal and let your pen glide across the page with the thought of Elizabeth or your own Wise Woman beside you, smiling encouragingly.

Interlude · Age 45

on the Cozy Landing, one perfect autumn afternoon

Ellie was snuggled up on the couch on the Cozy Landing, the inner place she returned to whenever her heart needed to catch its breath. It was a late October afternoon. Chase was a year older now, and Ellie was sitting with her journal, recording and relishing her many victories. She suddenly felt something inside her. It wasn't dread, but it was something like it. She stopped and said out loud, "I feel weird right now." She looked back at her journal and reread what she had just written. Maybe there was a clue there.

But all she saw was an ever-growing list of wins and things she was grateful for. Why was she feeling something negative? Where was it coming from? Ellie took a deep breath and closed her eyes. "Elizabeth," she said. "Elizabeth?"

When she opened her eyes, Elizabeth was there. She was sitting next to Ellie on the couch with a warm smile on her face.

"My darling Ellie," Elizabeth said. "It is so good to see you!"

Ellie smiled.

"I see your journal is open," Elizabeth continued, pointing at what was now the fourth volume. "Lots of good things in there."

Ellie looked down again at the pages. "Yes, but I have a really weird feeling right now. I'm not sure what's going on."

"Tell me more, " Elizabeth replied.

"Well, I was just sitting here writing down how well things are going. Chase is doing so much better at school. Joe and I are in a great rhythm. I got a promotion at work. I've got great friends and a great life. But I suddenly got a feeling in the pit of my stomach. It's like something bad is about to happen. I don't understand it. I don't understand what's going on."

"As far as you're aware, is something bad about to happen?" Elizabeth attentively asked.

"No," Ellie replied. "Nothing. I mean, we have our ups and downs, but nothing that would make me feel such …"

"Foreboding?" Elizabeth asked.

"Yes! That's it," Ellie replied. "It's like I'm waiting for the other shoe to drop. It's like I'm used to things going wrong, and something bad is just bound to happen."

"Ah, I understand," Elizabeth said. "That's a bit of a tough one."

Ellie put down her pen, closed her journal, and turned toward her faithful friend.

Elizabeth began. "Maybe it feels strange to you that things are going well. When you've lived with pain and uncertainty for so long, the good can feel unfamiliar or even suspicious. Part of you may even be waiting for the wheels to fall off, wondering when the old patterns will return."

Ellie listened. "That feels true," she said after thinking about it. "Can you help?"

"Well, if that's what's happening, and it sounds like it is, then yes, I can definitely help."

Ellie opened her journal and picked up the pen.

"We must learn how to *trust ourselves*," Elizabeth said. "You see, you've worked hard to rebuild your foundation from the ground up across your whole life. Now you are at this moment where good things are normal. It's new for you to live like this.

"As you acclimate to this updated version of your life, your beautiful brain sees it as unfamiliar and, on some level, sees it as a threat.

We are comfortable with what we know. The more you get to know this new life you've built, the more comfortable you will become.

"It's hard to accept your ability to shape what comes next in your life. You now have the strength and freedom to heal, grow, and make changes that lead to great outcomes. It might not feel quite natural yet, but you are living in your HeartPrint.

"I guess what I am saying is that you are not standing on *borrowed* ground. This is your life. It's time to live in it fully. So, I want you to try this any time you feel this sense of unease. Put your right hand here," she said, placing her right hand on her heart.

Ellie did the same. She felt her heart thumping reassuringly.

"Then, put your left hand down here," she continued, placing her left hand near her belly button.

Ellie did the same again.

"Then," she said, "Say this:

I am safe.
I am living the life I have always dreamed of.
This is all new to me, so it's a bit unfamiliar.
But it is here, and I am safe."

Ellie repeated each phrase. She noticed the feeling began to go away, replaced by the steady rhythm of her HeartPrint guiding her forward. She made note of her physical heart, which had never let her down either. She suddenly felt profoundly grateful for her physical body that allowed her to be here, to wrap her arms around her Loved Ones, and to experience all the pleasures life had to offer.

The Third Part

Awakening

Remembering

Becoming

Chapter 14 · Age 48

Paradise Funeral Home in Fiskdale, Massachusetts, sitting in an uncomfortable seat—the pain of loss

"I didn't know the deceased personally, but from what I have gathered, she was a fine woman …"

The preacher was halfway through his eulogy. Ellie sat in the front row with Joe and Chase. Her father and her brother, James, sat nearby. The small audience was scattered around the small room. Ellie sighed. Although she had cried when her mom was diagnosed with pancreatic cancer and had wept at her bedside as she watched her mother deteriorate, there were no tears now. There was only impatience. She wanted this part to be over.

The preacher finally finished, and the man from the funeral home walked slowly to the front. "On behalf of the family, we would like to thank all of you for attending. This concludes our service," he said solemnly, like he had hundreds of times before.

Those gathered stood up, and the sound of quiet conversations filled the room. There was no reception. There was no wake. Ellie found and hugged James. Although they hadn't been in close touch in recent years, there was the mutual affection of shared triumphs and tragedies that only siblings have.

"I love you so much," Ellie said softly to James as they embraced.

"Love you, Sis. With all of my heart," James said back.

Ellie gave her father a perfunctory hug.

"I loved your mother," he said.

"I know you did," Ellie replied, wanting to keep the conversation as short as possible. "Will you be heading out today?"

"Yes, back to Dorchester. I have work on Monday."

"Well, Dad, be safe," Ellie said as he walked away.

"Aunt Grace!" Chase, now 16 years old, interrupted the dour mood with enthusiasm.

"How is my favorite nephew?" Grace asked warmly, giving hugs to Chase, then Joe, and finally, Ellie.

"Thanks for coming," Ellie whispered.

"Love you so much," Grace said back. "Let's get together next week. I miss you."

"Of course," Ellie replied. "I'll call you."

It was a mostly quiet drive back to New Haven. Chase talked about his upcoming driver's license test. There were discussions about schedules, upcoming trips, and used cars.

Joe knew that Ellie would talk about the day's events in her own time and place. He instinctively knew a "normal" car ride home was what his wife wanted. At different times, he had sat by her side as she wept, and he had listened patiently to the stories of her childhood even though he had heard them many times before. As Ellie grew into her HeartPrint, both Joe and Chase benefited. Ellie was grateful that she was in a mostly warm and affectionate marriage. She realized it even more today as she thought about her disruptive childhood.

The only mention of Ellie's mom was when Chase asked what food Ellie's mom had liked best. "Chicken fried steak," Ellie said. They all laughed. Chase got out his phone and found a place on the way home that served his grandma's favorite dish. They stopped there for dinner, arriving home just as the summer sun set.

Ellie woke up early the next morning. While Joe and Chase slept, she made tea and sat down at her favorite place in the living room.

She sighed deeply and opened her journal. She flipped through the pages until she came to a part that said "Mom" in large, underlined letters. She scanned what she had written over the last three months.

It was so fast, she thought to herself.

The first entry started with, "Mom—cancer." She saw her notes about how severe and fast-moving pancreatic cancer was. She rubbed her fingers over the tear stains on the pages.

"I feel guilty" were the next words that caught her attention. She continued to read.

Ellie's Journal

Things I wish Mom had done differently:

- *Been more attuned to me when I was a kid*
- *Not been so selfish after the divorce*
- *Provided more stability when I was in high school*
- *Not had so many boyfriends*
- *Been a better grandma to Chase*
- *Learned to be a better listener*

Things I'm grateful for:

- *She was never abusive (like Dad could be)*
- *She let James and me live with her when Dad left town (same high school for four years!)*
- *She was with me when Chase was born (support)*
- *She accepted Joe*
- *Our last few years were pretty good …*

As she read the last words, she remembered the lunches they'd started having together every month or so. She was grateful her mom had tried harder as the years went on.

Ellie thought about Elizabeth. She closed her eyes, half expecting to hear her voice.

"I miss you, Elizabeth," she whispered.

"I've missed you, too."

Ellie looked and saw Elizabeth sitting in the chair next to the couch. She was leaning forward and dressed in black. Her black-rimmed glasses were perched low on her nose as she studied Ellie's face with a familiar warmth. She sat quietly, waiting for Ellie to speak.

"I'm so glad to see you!" Ellie said.

"Now, now, child," Elizabeth said. "Calm down. You'll wake the boys," she said with a small, knowing smile playing on her lips.

Holding her journal, Ellie scooched across the couch to be near her Wise Woman. "Where have you been?" she asked.

"Well, you've been doing so well," Elizabeth began. "I've watched you grow and change and become such a great mom and wife. And I'm so proud of who you are. You know I've always been right here with you."

"Thank you," Ellie said, "I couldn't have done it without you."

"Well," Elizabeth said. "We *are* a great team. And I'll always be here for you. You've done a lot of good work, and you've reaped the rewards. I'm glad to have been a part of the story. I'll bet it feels great."

Ellie thought back on how far she had come. "Yes," she said, "my life feels good most of the time. But I'm having a tough time ..." her voice trailed off.

"Mom?" Elizabeth asked simply.

"Yeah," Ellie said. "I can't seem to organize these feelings. It seems like my sadness is just a complicated bundle of emotions that come at the strangest times."

"I'd like to understand," Elizabeth said. "Tell me more."

Ellie was once again grateful to open up to her friend. "It's just that even though she wasn't the best mom and she made mistakes and kind of screwed me up, she did try to do better. And she *did* do better, and we got closer toward the end, but then she went so fast," Ellie blurted out.

They sat quietly together for a moment, letting everything sink in.

They talked some more. Ellie recounted her journal entries, talking about the confusion and pain she felt. Elizabeth listened closely but didn't say anything. Ellie finished and let out a long, deep sigh.

"I'm so sad for you," Elizabeth said.

Ellie and Elizabeth wept.

Elizabeth removed her glasses and wiped her eyes.

"Look at the two of us," she said. "We're a mess."

They both smiled.

"Well," Elizabeth said, "Here's what I know about grief."

Ellie looked at her expectantly.

"I heard about a farmer who bought a field. In the middle of the field, there was a big hole next to a giant tree. The hole was too big to fill in with dirt and too large to build anything over it. For a while, the farmer was angry. The hole was taking up space where crops could have been planted. He tried to ignore it, but every time he plowed the field, he had to swerve around it.

"Finally, he made a decision. He carried stones from the fields and placed them around the edge of the hole. Then, each day, he would carry buckets of water from his well and pour them into the hole. Eventually, the hole became a small pond.

"First, the birds came and bathed in it. Next, he noticed that deer made it a gathering place. Wildflowers sprang up around it as he kept the pond full, and eventually, his grandchildren built a swing in the tree nearby and would play in the shade. The hole never went away, but it somehow became useful and even beautiful."

Elizabeth paused. "I think that's how grief is. It doesn't go away. It will always be in the middle of your field. But we can choose how we live around it. And I think eventually, if we let it, it can even hold beauty for us."

They sat again in silence.

"This is going to take some time," Ellie said. "And it really *hurts*. It feels confusing, and that is scaring me. It reminds me of how painful and alone I have been because of her."

"Yes," Elizabeth replied. "Be patient with yourself. Grief doesn't keep a schedule, and your deep feelings show how important your mom is to you. You are becoming a better version of yourself. The kindest way to honor your mom is to use the pain to build something new—to grow from the pain."

Ellie smiled. "Thank you. This has meant so much to me. When will I see you again?"

"Maybe soon," Elizabeth replied. "Maybe in a while. Maybe never. But I think you know I'm already with you all the time and everywhere. Now," she said, "If I'm not mistaken, I hear Chase. He probably wants your Sunday breakfast special."

"The hole never went away, but it began to hold beauty."

From Elizabeth

Losing someone close to us is hard. Of course, Ellie had a lot of conflicted feelings. Maybe you've faced a loss like this in your life. If you haven't, you almost certainly will. Facing something like this is different from the challenge of your steady, day-to-day growth into your HeartPrint. It is traumatic, devastating, and sometimes sudden. We're left to navigate life without someone who once filled so much of it, holding the mix of love, hurt, and memory that remains.

I've heard that grief is the universal human emotion because it is something we will all experience. That makes sense. But it's also a unique experience each time because of the nature of the loss and how each of us processes it. Grief is a powerful and, at times, overwhelming feeling.

And grief isn't limited just to when someone close to us dies. It can happen with any kind of loss. Maybe it's losing a job or when a close friend moves away. Maybe a child moves out of our home. All of these things can bring grief.

Grief shows up in our lives in many ways. There is an emotional side to it. There's also a physiological side. This unique pain can be both acute and unrelenting. It can be bewildering. It can be so powerful that it may seem as if we may never have the ability to feel anything else again.

Our Western culture is not known for its open conversation about grief, particularly death and dying. Dying has been viewed as something that should be done out of sight, often shrouded in mystery. I'm glad that seems to be changing. We have begun to show more of a willingness to talk about death, incorporate rituals, and support people as they die.

I read a book that was written in 1969 by Elisabeth Kübler-Ross. It's called *On Death and Dying*. That's where the whole "stages of grief" thing came from. You probably know them. They are denial, anger, bargaining, depression, and acceptance.

That's a helpful place to start. But for anyone who has experienced grief, we know it usually doesn't follow a neat, linear process. We may find ourselves in one stage of grief for quite some time before we are ready to move on to the next stage. We might find ourselves going back and forth multiple times.

Maybe a *Shadow Sister* or two (or twelve!) shows up, and we get triggered, even after a long time has passed since the loss happened.

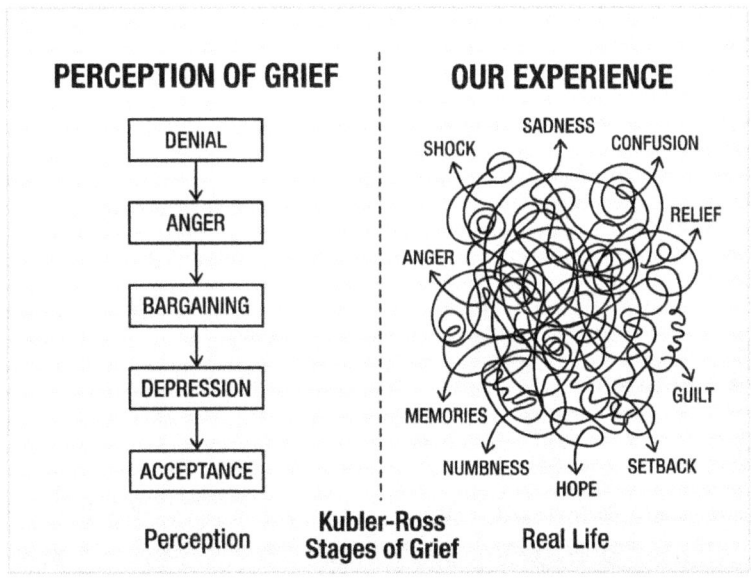

Grief is not a neat, linear process.

Grief can be like a roller coaster. It does loop-de-loops and takes unexpected turns and detours. Our grief can be unruly and unpredictable, and the feelings are usually negative and painful. They can stop us from living a normal life.

This happened to Ellie. Her grief eclipsed everything else for a time. It was consuming and overwhelming. It was hard to simply be *with* her grief. The pain was so intense that she didn't want to "give it time." She just wanted it to be over.

It wasn't in the story, but there were times when her *Angry Self* raged. She tried pushing the pain down and "just moving on." It didn't feel like she would ever gain her equilibrium again. Looking back on it now, I knew that the intense grief would eventually pass. But in the moment, it felt permanent to Ellie.

Like I told Ellie, I sometimes think of grief as a hole in the middle of the field of our lives. When it's first discovered, it feels bothersome, frustrating, and hopeless. But as time goes on and we approach our loss differently, the hole begins to be transformed. It never goes away, but our lives do go on. Our good relationships add to the transformation of the hole. New endeavors also add to it. The hole is always with us, but as we grow around it, it takes up less room. It can actually become a source of strength and beauty for us.

Just because we continue with life doesn't mean we have dealt with our grief. Just like all of the other big feelings, it is only dealt with when it is dealt with. The feelings must be externalized and processed one by one. And with big complicated experiences like grief and loss, we often need to process layers and layers over time. Grief can come in waves when you least expect it. If you are facing something like this, please don't lose hope or patience. Working through grief can take a long time. And, as we will see, it might come up even years later.

I want to take a little extra time with this subject because, as a culture, we don't really teach people how to grieve. Ellie didn't know how to grieve because she had never seen anyone do it. When her beloved grandmother died, Ellie's mother wasn't able to help her make sense of what was happening. That absence of support left a void, and in the vacuum of confusion, Ellie's beautiful brain interpreted the loss of her grandmother as a threat. It's hard to learn something like this if we've never seen it modeled or taught.

So, I would like to share some of the things that did help Ellie eventually manage the loss of her mother. The first word I would like to share is *partnership*. If we can view our loss as a partner we can learn from, we are off to a good start. Grief is not the enemy. We can look at our loss like an emotional stethoscope. It allows us to listen to our deepest feelings and understand ourselves more clearly. It may sound impossible to see the positives from our grief, but it is possible.

The next word is *attunement*. We've talked about this before. Try to become aware and identify the emotions you are feeling. Grief is a big word that contains a lot of other words like anger, guilt, shame, or even relief. Sit with your grief. Make room for your feelings and let them breathe. Your journal can really help. Meet these feelings with curiosity and explore them in detail.

Finally, very importantly, there is *self-compassion*. Your Wise Woman will accept your feelings no matter what the *Shadow Sisters* say. Don't judge your emotions; embrace them. As a part of self-compassion, accept that there will be times when you might feel overwhelmed. There might be days when you can't get out of bed, and that's okay.

Don't feel like you have to keep going full steam ahead. You might feel that you must because you feel like "it's required of me." Or you might want to move forward as a welcome distraction from your pain. If you do that, be careful. The feelings have not gone away. They will continue to affect you until you acknowledge them, accept them, and work through them. Grief can lead us either away from our HeartPrint or toward it.

One last thing. It's a warning about those kindhearted people who try to help during your grief. Beware of phrases like these:

"You'll get over it."
"You need to be strong."

And beware of things you tell yourself, like:

"I can't continue."
"I have nothing left to live for."

When these kinds of thoughts come up, the first step is to attune to them. Give yourself some space. Sit with the thoughts and be curious about them.

Then, ask yourself a simple question: Is this feeling I have really true?

Don't just ask the question and give a cursory answer. Take some time to think it through. Give it the space it deserves.

If you look closely, you'll see that most of the time these are "should" statements.

I should be able to get over this.

I should be able to stop feeling this way.

I should be strong.

Here's a new way to think about "should" statements. They are wishes. What you are really saying is:

I wish I could get over this.

I wish I could stop feeling this way.

I wish I could be strong.

Once we embrace the idea that "shoulds" are wishes, it gives us the ability to externalize them and respond to ourselves with compassion and validation. Of course you wish you were stronger. Of course you want the feelings to go away. It's normal to feel the intense pain of loss. It's a marker of how important this person or experience was to us, and it shows the deep love you have that now has nowhere to go.

When we view our feelings as wishes, it allows us to see, hear, and understand *ourselves* more clearly. It gives us the room to attune to these emotions and the information they bring. We can then begin to comfort ourselves as we process the experiences. Each time we do, we can close a browser tab and find some genuine and lasting relief.

Finding relief from the intense pain of grief is important. You and your Wise Woman may not be able to do it on your own. If you are having trouble, you can always turn to a trusted friend or a therapist. The important thing, as always, is to externalize your feelings, give yourself some room to feel them, and then process them.

Okay, I'm done. I hope it was worth your time to consider those thoughts.

I believe there are gifts in all of the emotions we experience, including grief. Maybe it's the recognition of how important that person or thing was to us. It might reveal how deeply we cared for someone or something. It provides an opportunity to connect with others. It allows us to evaluate our lives and consider if it's time to move in a new direction.

Ellie mostly did well as she worked through the feelings about her mom. And like all difficult relationships with parents, she had her ups and downs. A couple of years later, something profoundly deep was revealed. She had to go to Italy to discover it.

A Cup of Tea with Meg

The death of Ellie's mom was a significant loss. Since Ellie didn't have a secure attachment to her mother, she spent most of her life yearning for a sense of safety. That meant when her mother passed away, her grief was complicated. She was angry and judgmental at times and wished things had been different. Elizabeth helped her through this complicated experience and shared some valuable insights about the subject. Here are some thought questions for you to consider:

- How do you feel about either the death or the potential death of a parent or someone you love? What does it bring up for you?
- What could you do to support yourself in preparing to process this experience?
- What do you think about the analogy about the hole? Can you relate to it? Have you planted and grown anything to soften and beautify this space in you?
- Think about a loss you have experienced. Did it follow a regular pattern or was it more convoluted? Was it complicated? Do you need any extra support or help with it? Who might be a good person to help you with this?

Chapter 15 · Age 50

in the Chapel of the Fallen near the beautiful wall of marbles, Anghiari, Italy

Following her mother's death, Ellie drew even closer to her husband, Joe. He provided support, encouragement, and sensitivity. She also drew closer to Grace, her best friend. Ellie and Joe would meet for dinners with Grace and her husband, Hank. Their circle of friends grew as Chase entered his final years of high school.

At one of the dinner parties, the idea of traveling to Europe came up. They all had a playful argument over the best place to visit. Ellie argued for Italy, where her mother's side of the family had its roots. She talked of the wine, the food, and the history.

As often happens with discussions like this, it came and went. Then, one afternoon a few months later, in the middle of a cookout at their house, Grace plopped a folder on the table. "Hank and I are going to Italy. Who's in?"

"Italy?" Ellie said excitedly.

"Yes—Italy," Grace replied enthusiastically. "It has everything. And, mon amie," she said, looking at Ellie, "the place I've chosen is near the village where your family first came from. Here's the itinerary. It includes golf, tours, shopping, and magnificent restaurants. We leave in two months. I've made copies for each of us. Who's in?"

Ellie grabbed one of the sheets and showed it to Joe. As excited as she was, she didn't know if Joe would be on board or not.

"It looks perfect," Joe said. "Think about it. My mom can come and stay with Chase, and we're both due some time off at work. And I know it's something you've wanted to do for a long time. We should do it."

"Really?" Ellie was beaming.

"Absolutely," Joe said, enjoying his wife's joy.

A short two months later, they were off on the trip. It was Ellie and Joe, along with Grace, Hank, and another couple from the group, Josh and Libby. They landed in Florence, got into their two rented vans, and headed to the villa 45 minutes southwest of the city. It was a beautiful country estate that was close to everything they had planned.

The first few days were spent together, exploring, eating, and drinking. Ellie was struck by how different the energy was in Italy. It brought her a new perspective. She felt more open. She lost track of which day of the week it was and immersed herself in her husband, her friends, and the new culture.

After a week, it was time for the men to go on a two-day golf trip. They packed up one of the vans with the clubs and luggage.

"Sorry, honey," Joe said as they were getting into the van. "This is a boys' trip. You and I will definitely get out on the course later."

"Have fun!" Ellie said, kissing Joe's cheek.

The men drove off, leaving Ellie, Grace, and Libby together. Libby was playful, funny, and easy to be around.

They stood in the driveway as the van disappeared. "Well," Libby said, "What will we *ever* do without them?" The three women looked at one another and burst out laughing.

"I've got a feeling we will figure *something* out," Grace said. "I think we start with the pool!" she shouted.

That evening, over a homemade dinner of *tagliatelle ai funghi porcini* prepared by Libby, they discussed their plans for the next couple of days.

"Well, as you know, I'd like to visit Anghiari," Ellie said. "I want to see the place where my great-grandparents grew up. If you guys are okay with it, I'd like to go there tomorrow morning."

"You should go," Grace said. "Libby and I will spend the morning here, sleeping in. Right, Libby?"

"Yes, I don't think I have slept enough," Libby said playfully. "Maybe we can go out to dinner together afterward?"

"Perfect," Ellie said. "Now, who's up for a glass of Chianti and some cards?"

Ellie woke to soft morning light spilling through the window. She smiled, drew a long breath, and felt the quiet promise of the day. A few minutes later, with coffee in hand and wrapped in her favorite sweatsuit, she was behind the wheel of the van, heading toward Anghiari, a half hour away.

As she rode through sunlit hills, she noticed the sun-kissed autumn leaves. Her thoughts turned to her mother. Ellie had untangled so much over the years, yet something about this pilgrimage stirred a restlessness in her that she couldn't name. It felt like a pebble in her shoe, usually unnoticed, but now pressing with each mile.

The small town was just waking up when she arrived. She parked the van on a side street, got out, and started walking around, absorbing the energy of the village. She stopped for a pastry and a second cup of coffee at an old cafe that was just opening for the day. She strolled through the town square, looking in the windows of the shops. She felt connected to her past. Maybe a woman from her family had once stood behind one of these counters, greeting neighbors with the same morning smile.

Eventually, Ellie came across a small chapel nestled between stone buildings. A weathered plaque read, *Chapel of the Fallen—1777*. The chapel was small, but it was designed to look like a much larger church.

Ellie walked to the door. She smiled when she found it open. Inside, the air was cool and still. The walls were adorned with multicolored precious marbles, highlighted by the random rays of the sun shining through the small slits of the chapel's windows. She absorbed the tranquility as she silently made her way toward the altar.

To the left, she noticed a few votive candles burning in a part of the chapel that lacked the benefit of sunlight. Ellie walked over to them, fished in her pocket for a Euro, and placed it in the votive box. She took one of the long matches lying there and struck it. In the brief moment of light, she noticed she wasn't alone.

Kneeling off to the side was a woman with a young girl next to her. Their bowed heads looked up at the light from the match.

"Mi dispiace," Ellie said softly, using one of the few Italian phrases she had learned for the trip. "I'm sorry."

"Americano?" the woman asked softly.

"Si, Americano," Ellie replied, smiling.

"Who you remember?" the woman asked, pointing to the match that was still burning.

Ellie looked at the match and shook it until it was extinguished.

"I'm remembering my mother, my grandmother, and my great-grandmother," she said. Then, realizing from the quizzical look on the older woman's face that the language barrier was real, she simply offered, *"Mia madre."*

The woman smiled and said, "Ah. We remember my mother too ... her *nonna* ... her grandmother."

The little girl started speaking excitedly in Italian.

"What is she saying?" Ellie asked, hoping the woman understood enough English to translate the child's delight.

The woman chuckled. "She say, 'My gramma make good *ciambella*.' We always stop after chapel to eat some. She excited about the *ciambella*."

The girl started speaking again in Italian, like she was reciting something from rote memory. It was in a singsong tone of voice.

"Hanno fatto tutto il possibile. Il resto tocca a noi."

Ellie cocked her head and locked eyes with the mother.

"She say," the woman continued, "something we say about our old people."

"Can you tell me what it is?" Ellie asked.

"*In inglese significa* … it means … 'They did all they could. The rest is up to us.'"

Ellie repeated the words. "They did all they could. The rest is up to us."

The mother and child bowed their heads again. Ellie stayed still for a long moment, the words echoing inside her. This more expansive and thoughtful perspective on past generations struck Ellie. It was so full of grace. Then, she felt something loosen deep in her chest.

Her thoughts went to her mother. She tried to place her mom into this new perspective. For so many years, Ellie had focused on the pain her mother had caused in her life. Yes, she was grateful for the good things, but in this moment, for the first time, she thought about her mother as a person, separate from their relationship. She began to think about the profound struggles her mother had endured.

She played the oft-repeated scene of her mother with her friends, telling them the *"that's not my baby"* story. In this sacred moment, Ellie was able to look beyond the pain and consider the possibility that there might have been more to it than her mother's cruelty. Maybe it was her mother's way of coping with the guilt surrounding her birth. Perhaps it was her mom trying to make sense of how her daughter had turned out so differently from her.

Another scene came to mind. Her mother used to say with disdain, "You remind me of your father." Ellie now contemplated that the reason might be her mom's distress about her inability to connect with her only daughter. Perhaps Ellie's very existence was a daily reminder of the deep wound her mother had felt because of her first husband's betrayal.

More fragments came. Her great-grandfather leaving his family for another woman. His suicide months later. The two-week search before they found his body. Ellie pictured the ripples of that loss and how it had carved its way through generations. Suddenly, her mother's long trail of boyfriends looked not like recklessness, but reaching.

A wave of compassion rose and broke within her. "She did all she could," Ellie whispered.

Ellie was overcome with sadness. She realized her mother was a woman who had lacked the skills and support to heal and grow into a more mature and wiser version of herself. She thought about how her mother had rarely lived in her HeartPrint. Ellie now understood her mother's life was all about living up to some external expectations. She considered for the first time that her mother couldn't have given her what she needed. She *couldn't* have given something she didn't have.

Ellie gripped the wooden rail in front of her, knees trembling. The weight of truth settled in, solid and merciful. Their relationship had been built on a faulty foundation, and she and her mother had never truly bonded in an "us against the world" kind of way. How could she and her mother ever have come back to a place they had never known?

She thought of Chase and how he'd found help and support to grow through his struggles. What if her mother had been given the same?

Then her grandmother's kind, steady, and patient face came to her. Ellie could see now how her grandmother had tried to fill in the gaps her daughter couldn't. And later, how she had poured that same love into Ellie herself.

A sob tore loose. They had all tried. They had cared. And still, it hadn't been enough. Not because of will or love, but because the tools didn't exist. Healing hadn't yet been learned in their family line. It wasn't within her mom's choice or power.

Ellie pressed a hand to her heart and breathed deeply. "They did all they could," she said again.

And for the first time, she truly believed it.

Ellie sank into a pew, trying to catch her breath. For so long, she had believed her mother had seen the damage and *chosen* not to change. Now she understood. Perhaps her mother had seen it, but simply hadn't known what to do about it. The realization felt both heavy and kind.

She thought of Elizabeth and the steady wisdom that had guided her toward her own HeartPrint. That teaching had given her what the women before her had never had: a way to transform pain into peace. And now, sitting in the quiet glow of the chapel, Ellie felt it. It was the end of something old, and the beginning of something whole. She was breaking a chain that was generations long.

They did all they could. The rest is up to us.

The words moved through her again, no longer as insight, but as truth. The anxiety that had followed her up the hill dissolved, replaced by a deep, quiet calm. She accepted her mother, not as the figure who had failed her, but as a woman doing her best with what she'd had. The chain was broken, yet the bond remained.

She felt an unexpected gratitude for her mother's passing. Death had given them what life could not: a space to meet within her own heart, beyond judgment and need. Then, Ellie had the thought that if her mother had been even a little different, a little better, things might have changed in ways that would have hidden Elizabeth from her. Perhaps the clarity and compassion that now lived inside her would never have taken root so early, or so deeply. What had once felt like an unfair inheritance now seemed, in some mysterious way, to have carried its own blessing.

After a deep sigh, Ellie rose and returned to the candles. She struck another match, this time lighting the candle.

"This is for you, Mom," she whispered.

Ellie's ritual was interrupted by the Italian mother. "*Buona giornata.* Have a nice day!" the mother said, smiling. The mother and daughter stood up and walked out of the chapel, holding hands. The little girl skipped beside her mother, light and carefree, already chattering about the pastry waiting for her. As Ellie watched them go, something stirred inside. The unguarded joy of that simple skip sparked a memory of herself long ago, when each day still held small wonders. She could now sense that same wonder stirring within her once more, ready to shape her life ahead.

Turning back to the candle she'd lit, Ellie watched its flame burn steady and bright. A new thought came to her about her future. Someday she might be a grandmother herself. She pictured Joe beside her, both of them laughing as they played with their grandchild while Chase and his wife prepared dinner. The image filled her with a tender joy. It was now a future lit by love rather than loss.

Finally, she turned and walked back toward the door of the church. The precious marbles embedded in the wall seemed even more beautiful than before. She stopped and basked in a bright ray of light that hit her face, making her close her eyes. She imagined it was her mom, her grandmother, and her great-grandparents loving her and willing her forward in her life.

As she approached the door, she saw a basket filled with marbles of different sizes sitting on a raised table. Next to it was a handwritten sign, folded to stand up. It said, *"Prendine una per chi porti nel cuore."* Ellie wasn't sure what it meant, but it seemed right to take one to remember this morning.

She searched through the basket until she found one that felt right in her hand. It was large and turquoise in color. She squeezed it, transferring the wisdom of this experience into the stone, so she would never forget. She solemnly placed it in her bra, close to her heart. It would forever honor the people who allowed her to be here and live this life. Ellie opened the door and stepped into the brilliant daylight of a small town that was now bustling with people.

"They did all they could. The rest belongs to us."

From Elizabeth

What a memory this is. It was a profound moment in Ellie's life. She experienced something that went beyond forgiveness.

Most of us are taught as children that forgiveness is important. When we hurt someone, the right thing to do is say we are sorry. Then, the person accepts our apology, and we continue with whatever we are doing. But there's much more to true forgiveness.

There is the first layer of forgiveness. That's when we say, "I forgive you." This means something. It shows an intention to let the situation go. It means you have a willingness to no longer hold it against the offending person. It's a great start.

But to live in our HeartPrint, there's another part to it. We have to somehow organize the confusion and pain surrounding the hurt. It has to make sense to our beautiful brain. That is another layer of forgiveness, and it takes time and work.

For Ellie, that didn't happen until she stood in the chapel. That morning, she understood, at a heart level, the *reality* of who her mother was. She had a sacred moment where she realized her relationship with her mom could never have been anything other than the way it had been. It had been all her mom had available to offer. If it could have been different, it would have been.

This was a real step of growth. Ellie finally *understood* her mother. She was able to organize her thoughts, which led to soothing her emotions. That day, Ellie became a new version of herself. The pebble in her shoe was gone. It had transformed into the turquoise marble that represented lineage with gratitude. It was a memento for all they had endured so she could be here. She realized she could now live a more peaceful, fulfilled life.

Forgiveness is a complex and difficult thing for all of us. It's easy to resist forgiveness out of a sense of justice. But when we don't forgive, we are the ones who get hurt. The offending person goes on with their life, and we are stuck. We're caught in the moment that hurts us, and the hurt continues.

It gives an opportunity for our *Shadow Sisters* to appear, who are always trying to protect us. They will help us justify and rationalize our feelings. It's a safer choice. As I've shared before, it's important to hear those voices. It's an invitation for us to work on *why* we hurt. It's a chance to attune, understand, heal, and grow. We didn't create the pain, but we are the ones who carry it and spill it over, onto our Loved Ones. So, it becomes our responsibility to heal.

Sometimes I think we minimize the hurts we have suffered. If we haven't been neglected or abused, we figure that whatever has happened to us is trivial. That's not the case. These "small hurts" can really affect the connection to our Wise Woman and our HeartPrint. For instance, as a child, Ellie was never struck by anyone in anger. However, she was often misunderstood, minimized, and ignored. She lacked the support of the exact people who were supposed to be there for her—her mom and dad. That opened a lot of browser tabs that needed to be resolved.

Here's something to consider: Have there been hurts in your life or even trauma that keep you from living in your HeartPrint? Maybe you were disrespected. Perhaps you were harmed, ignored, or insulted as a child. It's possible you were treated differently because you were a girl. There's a chance your opinions didn't count as much as those of your brothers.

Things like this do have a significant impact. They undermine our connection to our inner wisdom because we think we somehow "should have" been able to stop it from happening. These experiences make living in our HeartPrint more difficult. We often live with things like regret, low self-worth, and blame-shifting.

The hurts of our childhood are the origin of our *Shadow Sisters*. Like Ellie, they are "pebbles in our shoe." We learn to live with them, but they change the way we walk. They don't hurt us until they do. And when they do, it hurts a lot. It takes us straight to the Basement of Shadows. From there, we are triggered, and we might hurt the ones we love by breaking our connection and trust with them. These hurts sometimes grow and can significantly damage our relationships. These pebbles always interrupt our ability to live a full life that feels good.

I have one last thing to share before we leave the topic of forgiveness. It has to do with big "T" trauma and little "t" trauma.

Little "t" trauma is what Ellie went through. It involves being mistreated. It is not something to brush aside. Until we work through the hurts, they can have a drastic effect on our relationships and happiness.

I also want to mention big "T" trauma. This includes things like sexual abuse, a family member's drug or alcohol addiction, domestic violence, losing a parent or caregiver in childhood, or family estrangement. These affect us differently. It can feel impossible to forgive this trauma because it affects our nervous system and our brain codes. It produces similar results to those that would occur if our life were in danger. How can we forgive someone for something like that?

If that is you, you may not be able to forgive on your own. Consider seeking the help of a professional. There are things like eye movement desensitization and reprocessing (EMDR) therapy or cognitive processing therapy (CPT) that can be very beneficial when trying to process and release big "T" traumas.

Sometimes, the best thing we can do for ourselves is to get professional help. We do it in other areas of life. When we have a legal question, we turn to an attorney. When our basement gets flooded, we call a plumber. Doesn't it make sense that if we've gone through big "T" trauma, we would call in someone who has been trained to help with that? It is possible to get on the other side of it with help.

The trip to Italy was a life memory for Ellie. She played golf with her husband on some beautiful courses. She drew closer to her friends. And she connected with her past. These were some great years for her. But, as you will see in the next story, there were still lessons to be learned.

A Cup of Tea with Meg

We dove deeper into the idea of forgiveness in this chapter. We explored how difficult some parts of it are. Here are some questions to help you:

- Why do you think it took Ellie's going to Italy before she could work through her deepest feelings about her mother?
- Which of your relationships have presented the biggest challenge to you in the area of forgiveness?
- What do you think about the big "T" and little "t" discussion? Which of those can you relate to the most? What steps might be available to you to help you work through the pebbles in your shoes?

Chapter 16 · Age 52

on a perfect spring day amidst the smell of jonquils in the Milford community garden

It was a beautiful spring Saturday morning, and Ellie sat at the kitchen counter thumbing through *Milford Happenings*, a local magazine that listed upcoming events. She daydreamed about what Chase might be doing. He had left for college seven months earlier, disrupting Ellie's day-to-day life. No longer were her days busy juggling her schedule with Joe's and Chase's. She wasn't asked to volunteer at the high school. Her high school connections with the other parents were quickly fading.

Ellie felt uncomfortable. The normal routines were gone. She would sometimes come into the kitchen on a weekday morning and absentmindedly open the refrigerator to prepare Chase's breakfast before realizing it was just her at home. Joe was fully engaged at work, so there were gaps in her day when she wasn't sure what she was supposed to do. She was still a successful manager at her company, but she had an uneasy feeling she couldn't seem to shake. Her work life was on autopilot. Her personal life often left her feeling unimportant and disengaged. She didn't know what life as an empty nester was supposed to feel like.

On the other hand, her relationship with Joe had grown steadily. They were close friends and understood each other. They had the kind of relationship that only years together can produce, but it didn't mean that Joe filled every hole in her life. This was a time of uncertainty.

She turned her attention back to the magazine just as Joe came into the kitchen.

"I'm going to go to the community garden today," she said as he poured a cup of coffee.

"It sounds like something an old person would do," Joe replied, smiling.

Ellie realized Joe was right. She had become the older person thumbing through free, local magazines looking for activities. Her younger self would have been judgmental. She turned the page and saw some younger people in the garden. She held up the magazine, showing him the picture. "Well, evidently it's for people of *all* ages," she said playfully.

Joe stopped and looked at it. "Well, you will find me on the golf course today. By the way, we are all set at the club to play next week with Grace and Hank."

"Great!" Ellie said. "But this is a bunch of *new* people," she continued, pointing at the magazine and imagining the awkward moments that come with being the new person. "And I don't know anything about gardening. Maybe it's a stupid idea."

"You'll never know if you don't try," Joe said, walking toward the garage. He knew Ellie was going to do this, and she was just working through her reservations out loud.

As Joe had anticipated and with much mental effort on her part, a little while later, Ellie threw a floppy hat she had purchased just for this reason onto the front seat, got into her car, and began the drive. She had seen the community garden many times before, promising herself to look into visiting it. Today was the day.

She arrived at the garden, parked the car, put on her hat, and walked toward her destination. She noticed a nagging pain in her hip as she walked. It had bothered her on and off for several months, but, as before, she set her concern aside. When she arrived, she saw there was only one other person there. It appeared to be an older man who was kneeling next to his section of the garden.

"Good morning," Ellie said politely.

"Well, good morning to you, Miss," the man said, standing up. "I'm Thomas." Thomas was indeed an older man; he was rotund, ruddy, and somewhat disheveled.

"I'm Ellie. It's nice to meet you," she said politely.

"Will you be joining our garden club today?" he asked with a bright smile on his face, looking right into Ellie's eyes.

"Well, I'm not much good at it," she said. "But I'd like to give it a try."

"Well, then, no time like the present. Let's get you started!" he said. He began walking. As Ellie followed behind, she noticed his rubber boots as they scraped across the ground.

"We have a perfect spot for you right over here," he said, pointing. "By the way, do you have any tools?" he asked, looking her up and down.

Ellie was flustered. *Tools? Of course, I need tools*, she thought. "Uh, I thought I would wait until later for that," she said.

Thomas stopped. "Well, here it is," he said, oblivious to her embarrassment. "I think you'll enjoy this one," he continued, pointing at her little piece of the garden. "Lots of sun."

"Thank you," Ellie replied.

"The rules of the garden club are simple, my dear," Thomas said. "Plant what you want. But nothing *illegal*," he said, smiling.

Ellie smiled back

"So," Thomas asked with genuine curiosity. "What *will* you be planting?"

Ellie had never even thought about that question.

"I'm not sure," she said. "Maybe some flowers and vegetables."

They stood there quietly for a minute. "Well, I have a shovel if you'd like to borrow it," Thomas said. "But you don't have any gloves. Gloves are important. We don't want those delicate hands to get blisters."

"No, that's fine," Ellie replied. "I'll get some before I come back again," she said. *If I come back again*, she thought.

"Well, you'll find there are a lot of nice people here," Thomas said. "Enjoy your garden!" Thomas left to go back to his work, leaving Ellie alone.

She stood there for a few minutes. She took a deep breath and looked around.

This is a really beautiful place, she thought. *I should give this a try.*

She watched as a few more people sauntered in and started working quietly on their particular plots. *Hmm … she thought. New people—ugh.* She began the trek back to her car.

"Hello," said the first woman she passed.

"Good morning," Ellie said, smiling.

That got the attention of a few more gardeners. Some of them stopped their work and stood up. Thomas stepped forward and said, "I'd like to introduce everyone to Ellie. She's *our newest community gardener,*" he said as if announcing a star player to a packed stadium.

Several hellos and welcomes came. *Well, I guess I'm in this now,* she thought.

Ellie smiled and waved to her fellow gardeners and continued toward her car. As she walked, she noticed a middle-aged woman who wasn't a part of the welcoming committee. The woman was on her knees, digging furiously with a hand trowel, her head down. She was grunting.

Something inside Ellie drew her to the woman. "Hello," she said, interrupting the woman's work. "I'm Ellie. I'm new here."

"Oh, I'm sorry. I was lost in my work. My name is Ree," she said, standing up and wiping her brow. "I'm afraid I don't have the right tools for this job."

Ellie looked at the woman's garden. She had barely made a dent in the soil. Then Ellie looked at her more closely. She was younger than Ellie and a bit shorter. She had long black hair and deep brown eyes. She was wearing black slacks, a pullover shirt with large yellow and black horizontal stripes, and a bright yellow baseball cap. Ellie smiled at how unique she was.

"Oh! A newbie like me," Ellie said warmly. "Well, at least you have a good sense of fashion." Ellie wasn't sure why she was teasing someone she had just met.

Ree laughed. "Yes, thank you," Ree replied jokingly, looking at herself. Then she smiled and said, "But I have you beat in the hat department."

Ellie pulled off her floppy gardening hat and looked at it. "I'll have you know that, according to *Garden Fashion Magazine, this* is the season's choice of headwear." Ellie laughed as their eyes met in the first bloom of friendship.

"I'll let you get back to work," Ellie concluded.

Ree smiled and got back on her knees, and Ellie watched as she continued to stab the ground furiously.

It's like she's a very productive and focused bumblebee, she thought. Ellie smiled again.

"Maybe I'll see you out here," Ree said, looking over her shoulder.

"It was nice to meet you," Ellie said.

She walked back to her car, relieved to be alone again, yet sure she would return.

"At least you have a good sense of fashion."

From Elizabeth

It was hard for Ellie when Chase went away to college. He had been such a part of her daily life that his absence had created a gaping hole. It made Ellie look at life in a different way.

When one thing ends, something new begins.

It was all a bit threatening. It wasn't *automatic* anymore. I think all of us love our routines. We pick up our keys from the same bowl, drive to the same store, and park in the same spot. It's comfortable.

But if we suddenly have to go to a new store, our nervous system engages differently. We have to use a different part of our thinking. Stress comes into play.

I'd like to share about something called System 1 and System 2 Thinking. It comes from a psychologist called Daniel Kahneman, in his book called *Thinking, Fast and Slow*. It helps explain what Ellie went through in her first garden adventure.

System 1 Thinking is the old routines and patterns we repeat daily. It's what we do on autopilot and doesn't take a lot of thought or analysis. It's made up of things like our instinct and intuition. When we are in System 1 Thinking, we make almost instantaneous decisions. It doesn't demand much energy or mental bandwidth from us. This is "thinking fast" in the book. We saw this when Ellie went to the fridge automatically to make breakfast for Chase, even though he wasn't there anymore.

System 2 Thinking is what happens when we face something new. The book calls it "thinking slow." We use this system when we are learning something new. It's when we need to use logic and rationale to help us make decisions. It's methodical, rational, and analytical. It goes through the available information for us to make the best decision.

How do you know when you are in System 2 Thinking? You ask yourself questions like these:

- What should I say?
- What should I do?

- Is this working?
- Do I need to make adjustments to this?
- Do I like how this is arranged?
- Do I need to arrange it differently?
- That didn't work. What should I do now?
- That didn't work either; what should I try now?
- It did work. What comes next?

Here's the tricky part. Our beautiful brains generally don't like to stay in System 2 Thinking for very long. By default, they want to stay in System 1. It's safer. It's comfortable and familiar. We don't have to be vulnerable, and we don't have to "come up with a plan." Remember, our brain's first job is to keep us safe.

Also, it takes extra energy to slow down and think. Then, it takes even more energy to implement a plan and stick with it. It's definitely a more conscious, energetic approach to life. Our beautiful brain uses a lot of energy already, so it tries to conserve what it can. Avoiding System 2 Thinking is an easy option. It's a way for our brain to stay safe and energized at the same time.

System 2 Thinking is, at its core, creation-based. It's where we build our lives intentionally. It allows us to unite and partner with our Wise Woman and move into our HeartPrint. Ellie has had to switch into this type of thinking many times in her journey so far, most recently when she decided to try out the gardening club. Our *Shadow Sisters* are a part of System 1 Thinking—they show up without an invitation. To get them off center stage, our thinking must be *slowed down*.

To put it simply, we must go slow before we can go fast.

When Ellie decided to go to the garden club, she first had to admit things weren't the same. She had to consider a lot of different options for how to face something new. Next, she had to choose one of the options and then formulate a plan. She had to get in the car and drive to the garden. She had to meet new people like Thomas, Ree, and the other gardeners. It was uncomfortable. She hadn't thought of everything, so she had to tolerate the distress and vulnerability of not remembering to bring tools and thinking about what to grow. As she looked back on it later, it was well worth the effort.

System 2 Thinking is the pathway to your Wise Woman and, ultimately, to living from your HeartPrint. It's the part of you that slows down, creates a little space, and lets you see a person, feeling, or situation with fresh eyes. System 2 is deliberate; it notices, questions, and chooses, which is exactly the posture your Wise Woman takes.

The encouraging part is that the more often you engage that slower, attuned way of thinking, the more it begins to reshape your System 1 Thinking. Over time, the Wise Woman's responses, which were once intentional and effortful, now start to arise on their own. What begins as practice becomes pattern, and those HeartPrint-aligned choices move from conscious effort into something far closer to instinct.

I'd like to invite you to notice your System 1 and System 2 Thinking as you move through your day, and up and down your stairs from your Basement of Shadows to your Beautiful Attic. What parts of your life are on autopilot? What are the things you do in your daily activities and relationships that really don't require much energy or thought?

These System 1 Thinking patterns can be helpful or unhelpful. If your pattern is to automatically thank someone when they have done something nice, that's a helpful pattern. If it's to avoid interactions with new people as much as possible, it's likely not as helpful.

As your browser tabs get closed, hopefully you will find energy to engage more and more in System 2 Thinking. And you will find yourself more and more attuned to your own beautiful HeartPrint.

Well, let's get back to the garden.

A Cup of Tea with Meg

At different times, we all have to face something new. It could be moving to a new place, making a significant purchase, or needing to make new friends. Recognizing the specific challenges around something new can help us navigate them in our HeartPrint.

- What life transitions have you experienced? Maybe it was middle school to high school, high school to college, or your first job. Think of times where things changed drastically, and the old system was no longer available.

- Can you think of examples of System 1 Thinking in your life?

- Have you faced any System 2 Thinking recently? What was it like?

- How can our Wise Woman help us in moments where things are very different for us than normal?

Chapter 17 · Age 52

back in the Milford community garden with a new friend

Two weeks later, Ellie made her way back to the Milford Community Garden for the third time. On her second trip, she asked Thomas for guidance and then tilled the soil, adding some fertilizer. She didn't see Ree.

It was another beautiful Saturday morning, and she was ready to plant some seeds. She wondered if she would see her newfound friend this time. Just in case, she filled her coffee thermos to the top and brought an extra cup. On her way out the door, she put a big blueberry muffin in a bag, picturing herself and Ree sharing it.

Parking in her usual spot, she began to walk back to her plot. Like before, she noted that her right hip was still hurting. She dismissed it again as "getting up there" in age. She looked at the gardens as she walked. Each one was so different.

She smiled when she saw Ree, hunched over and toiling away with a hoe. Ellie watched her take the short, choppy swings. She was wearing the same outfit as the first time they'd met.

My bumblebee, she thought.

"Good morning, Ree!" Ellie said. "Have you been here long?"

"I got here early," Ree replied. "I don't think I was cut out to be a gardener. Look at this," she huffed, pointing to her mangled plot and wiping her brow.

"Well, any shortcomings are certainly not from a lack of effort," Ellie said warmly.

Ree stood up straight, leaned on her hoe, and looked at Ellie. Ree found she naturally trusted Ellie.

"I come here because it helps me work out my frustration," she said, tapping the ground with the hoe. "My boss is crushing me with work," she continued. "My son is having trouble in school. And I just don't have any way to relieve the stress." Once she started talking, she wanted to say even more. "I tried talking to him, but it didn't seem to do any good," she continued.

Ellie wasn't sure who "him" was, but simply answered, "That must be hard."

Ree was relieved to have her words met with compassion. She dropped her hoe on the ground. Ellie could tell she was close to tears. She thought a muffin and a cup of coffee might be helpful.

"Why don't we sit for a minute?" Ellie asked.

Ellie walked toward a nearby bench, and Ree followed. Ellie sat down and patted the seat next to her.

"I brought you something," Ellie started. She pulled the muffin out of the bag, broke it in half, and gave the big half to Ree. Then she pulled out her thermos and poured them both a cup of coffee.

"Cream with a little sugar?" Ellie asked.

"This is so perfect," Ree replied. "I'm starving."

They sat quietly for a moment, eating their breakfast. Then Ellie spoke up.

"I know a little about bosses … and sons," she said. "If you want, you can tell me about it."

Ree started talking almost as furiously as she gardened. Everything came out quickly and unvarnished. Ellie nodded, touched Ree's hand, laughed, and occasionally shook her head. It was like a faucet that couldn't be turned off.

Finally, Ree concluded with, "And I just don't have anyone I can talk to about it."

"Well, my friend, you do now," Ellie said quietly.

There was an energetic silence. It was the kind of silence that happens when two people have connected in a real way. No one was groping for words; they were simply absorbing the moment.

Finally, Ellie said, "Well, those are certainly some big challenges." She thought back to her times with Elizabeth. *What would Elizabeth say here?* she wondered.

"I think it's great you are taking time to come here," Ellie began. "That's important. I think you are strong enough to figure this out. I know it's painful and confusing right now. You just have to take it one thing at a time."

"I don't feel … *strong*," Ree replied with her head down.

Again, there was the comfortable silence of contemplation.

"What if you and I had lunch together today?" Ellie said. "I live just a few minutes away."

Ree sighed. "I wish I could," she replied, "but duty calls. I have to finish a report for work by Monday. Maybe I can buy you a cup of coffee later this week?"

"I do love conversing over coffee … or tea …" Ellie said thoughtfully. "Definitely. Let me get your number."

Ree stood up. "Thanks, Ellie," she said sincerely.

Ellie could tell she was calmer now. "Of course," she replied. "Now take it easy on that poor garden."

Ree laughed. "It doesn't stand a chance against me!" she said, grabbing her hoe and holding it up to the sky.

Ellie stood up stiffly, her hip protesting the movement, and with a slight limp, resumed the walk toward her garden. On the way, she noticed a bee landing on a beautiful flower. She stopped and watched. She thought about how the bee needed the flower, and the flower needed the bee. She thought about how the flower needed the ground, and the ground needed the flower. She smiled and thought about Ree.

Then she thought about Elizabeth and all of the help she'd received from her. She looked forward to giving away what she had gained, like she had with Chase. But this was different. Ellie was ready to play her small part in strengthening the life of her newfound friend.

"The bee needs the flower, and the flower needs the bee."

From Elizabeth

I like this one. It shows how much Ellie had grown. She had reached the place where she had the capacity to invest in someone besides her family and close friends. She made a great connection with Ree that day. I like how brave and confident Ellie was. She noticed someone who needed help and was both willing and able to help. There was something special about sharing wisdom with her newfound friend.

There was a time when sharing wisdom was generational. An older person shared with their child, who in turn shared with their child. But it's not like that as much anymore. I understand it's still there, and I hope you have it. I know there are many of us who don't. So, we must take steps to supplement what is missing.

I think it's important that we share our wisdom with others and have them give their wisdom to us. It's a universal need. I love how Ellie was able to share with Ree what had been given to her. When we do that with one another, the world becomes a better place. Everyone wins.

Ree ended up becoming a close and long-term friend. She made it through her crisis, even though she ended up getting divorced. Ellie and Ree went through a lot together in the next two decades. They shared laughter, tears, and mutual comfort. It became one of Ellie's most special relationships.

Ellie ended up making the garden a part of her life. She went back every year to plant, water, and watch things grow. There was something reassuring and connective about the experience. It reminded her of how life really works.

Well, that ends the Third Part. It's time to skip ahead a full 10 years, to the Last Part. I wish we had the time to talk about all of the wonderful, scary, traumatic, and triumphant things that happened. I wish I could tell you more about Ree, Grace, Joe, and Chase. But alas, time doesn't allow it. We must fast-forward.

A Cup of Tea with Meg

Wisdom shared is wisdom gained. Wouldn't it be great if we all both gave and received wisdom from those around us? Really doing that can be a challenge.

- What keeps us from sharing the wisdom we have with others?
- How can we invite others to give their wisdom to us?
- How can we receive others' wisdom in a way that allows us to sift, sort, and pick up the pieces that truly serve us and our unique HeartPrint?
- What does sharing wisdom have to do with living in our HeartPrint?

The Last Part

Awakening → Remembering → Becoming → Embodying

Chapter 18 · Age 63

at the Apple Orchard Golf Course on another beautiful autumn day—touching the divine

Ellie opened the door to the garage and walked toward her bag of golf clubs. It had been five months since she had played. That's the rule when you've had a total hip replacement.

The pain in her right hip that she had first noticed in the community garden all those years ago had grown steadily worse. After MRIs, cortisone shots, and physical therapy didn't work, it was clear she needed surgery. The weeks leading up to the surgery were difficult. Ellie was in pain most of the time.

She was still expected to be a wife, employee, friend, neighbor, and mom. The combination of her physical pain and the expectations of others compounded over time. She felt her resentment and frustration grow as she seemed to continually fall short of expectations and disappoint people.

She had felt for years now that she was living in her HeartPrint most of the time. But recently, that sense of daily confidence had waned. She didn't like that her health was in the hands of doctors, nurses, and insurance companies that she didn't know. She didn't like the risks of surgery, including blood clots, pulmonary embolisms, and infections. For the first time in a long time, she contemplated the ultimate "what if" of death. Her *Shadow Sisters'* voices started showing up more and became harder to move off center stage. As her pain increased, Ellie began to break connections with the people she loved and liked. She went onto the wrong side of the Stress Curve. Chronic pain will do that.

She began to break familiar patterns. She didn't do things like immediately returning Chase's texts. She turned down invitations for dinner and tea with friends. But mostly, it showed up in her relationship with Joe. Ellie became more and more isolated. Her *Shadow Sisters* began to clamor for control. Her *Angry Self, Inner Critic,* and *Blame-Shifting Self* all made appearances. She was generally unhappy for the first time in years.

Finally, the time came for the operation. She received a brand-new hip after three hours of surgery. The doctor declared it a success, but it was hard for Ellie to appreciate it because of all the pain she was in. She was never one to take drugs, but now, the oxycodone was needed. It made her groggy, forgetful, and easily irritated.

Once home, she was very dependent on Joe. Joe was kind, but nurturing and caretaking were not a part of his HeartPrint. Ellie became resentful when Joe didn't take care of her the way she wanted him to. Instead of addressing her feelings and processing them, she became short and snippy with him. Their interactions mostly consisted of her complaining about her pain, her doctor, her physical therapist, and her lack of bowel movements. She was hard to be around.

One day, Joe sat down on the couch next to her. He tried to engage in a conversation about how she was doing. Over the past several years, they had established a solid pattern of communication, but the most recent events had disrupted it. Ellie saw he was trying to say and do the right thing, but she would only give short answers. She didn't want to talk about it.

As part of the recovery from her surgery, she was required to go on short walks around the house, at first with a walker and later, a cane. "This is stupid," she often said out loud. Joe did his best to attend to her and support her, but he mostly stayed out of her way.

After one of her treks, she made her way back to the recliner and sat down. She glanced at the bookshelf nearby. She wanted to reread one of her favorite novels, *The Night Circus* by Erin Morgenstern. She couldn't reach the book without getting up, so she leaned backward and grabbed her cane, which was leaning against the wall. She was just able to reach the bookshelf with it.

"Come to me, dearest Erin," she said out loud, using the end of her cane to nudge the book free. She then placed the handle on top of the book and carefully pulled it toward her. When she did, two books came flying onto the floor. One was the novel. The other was a book she hadn't opened for years. She picked up both of them. She set the novel aside and looked at the other book. There, covered with a smattering of dust, was the first journal she had completed 20 years earlier.

She wiped off the cover, opened it to a random page, and started reading.

"I tripped on a tree root," it began.

She paged through the journal, reading all of the feelings she had gone through years ago when Chase was having trouble in school. She saw "Miss Keene" written in large letters with a big heart drawn next to it. Her notes recounted her feelings, how she had processed them, and then how she had resolved them one by one.

She spotted her early notes from the first conversation with Elizabeth on the Cozy Landing. The word *HeartPrint* stood out, a question mark scribbled beside it. Ellie smiled, a sense of satisfaction settling over her. Scattered across the pages were other phrases like "Stress Curve," "Browser Tabs," and "Feelings Wheel"—reminders of how far she'd come. She saw the first time she'd written the words *Shadow Sisters*.

As she went through the journal, her emotions rose and fell. Disappointed at times and elated at others, she was reminded of the journey she'd taken two decades earlier.

An hour later, she got to the last page. She sighed deeply and thought about what she would do next. The answer was clear.

"Joe!" she shouted.

"Yes, dear?" Joe replied from the other room.

"I can't wait to go golfing with you."

Joe walked into the room. "What?" he asked.

"I've been thinking," she said. "And I can't wait for us to go golfing again. I miss that."

Joe squinted his now older eyes, confused. Was his wife making peace? He sat down next to her.

"I'm sorry, Joe," she started. "I haven't been my best for a while now, and I know that. You've been nothing but sweet and kind, and I've been nothing but difficult. Can you forgive me?"

Joe smiled. "Thanks," he said. "Of course, I forgive you. I know how hard it's been. I hate how things have been between us. It's made me appreciate what we built before. I'm just not very good at this stuff," he finished, waving his hand at all the medical equipment scattered around.

"Well, I found this," Ellie said, holding up the journal. "I guess I had forgotten what got us to where we are …" Her voice trailed off. She looked at her husband and said, "I will do better. I will be better. I love you and I appreciate you. I'm sorry I took you for granted."

Joe took her hand. "And I love you, Ellie," he said. "It won't be long before we are back on the course. I've missed that."

"Yes," Ellie said with a smile, "soon."

During the next few weeks, Ellie began journaling again. She explored her big feelings without judgment and summoned the spirit of Elizabeth. She called out the *Shadow Sisters*, who had become more prominent recently.

She wrote, "My *Angry Self* said those mean things to Joe. She was just trying to help, but I need to be grateful for what he's doing and not so easily angered. I think my anger gave me the feeling that I was in some kind of control."

She resolved to embrace the recovery period. She decided it was an opportunity to read and spend time with her husband. She started reaching out to Chase. She invited Grace and Ree over to watch a movie.

Ellie also wrote about what her hip replacement meant to her in facing her own mortality. She realized that were it not for modern medicine, she wouldn't be where she was. Her anger, confusion, and disconnection began to be replaced with something like gratitude, but much deeper. Ellie reconnected to Elizabeth and then, finally, to her HeartPrint. Things got much better then, and Ellie was grateful most days for her ability to remember those early lessons from Elizabeth.

※ ※ ※ ※

Six Saturdays later, the time finally came, and it was time to golf with Joe. Ellie was anxious and excited. She retrieved her golf clubs from the garage and brought them to the car. Joe wasn't far behind. They met Grace and Hank, drove together to the course, loaded their clubs onto the golf cart, and started their long-awaited round. Ellie was excited to be in the same cart as Grace, and from the beginning, they engaged in a warm conversation about her hip, their families, and their futures.

It was the fifth hole where it happened. Ellie wasn't playing well, but she was having a great time. The four of them made the same jokes they had made dozens of times before, laughing like it was the first time they had heard them.

They walked up to the tee, and Ellie was the last to hit her drive. She hit it decently, and it landed in the fairway. She hopped into the cart and scooched closer to Grace. They started down the hill on the cart path, heading for their next shot. There was a view of a beautiful lake below them. On their right, the trees swayed in the wind. The sun cast a dramatic shadow over the course.

Ellie became deeply aware of the blessing she was experiencing. She realized that if she were her grandmother's age, she would not have been able to have her hip replaced. She would have been relegated to a life of pain, managed only by drugs. Then she considered that she could have died from a blood clot, embolism, or infection. Her sense of gratitude grew deeper.

She realized that she was able to do something people born in previous generations could never have done: get the gift of 20 more years of a healthy hip. She thanked God for all of the doctors who had developed the surgery over the years. She quietly honored all of the thousands of patients who had gone before her, enduring those doctors' experiments on hip replacements to perfect the procedure. She was grateful to live in a country where the best surgery was available and to have the financial means to have the operation.

She did some quick math and realized she had been given another thousand rounds of golf with her friends. She acknowledged the profound gift of her own agency and the new lease on life it had given her.

"Elles," Grace interrupted her thoughts. "It's your turn."

Ellie got out of the cart, grabbed her 5-iron, and walked toward her ball.

She looked at Grace and said, "Get your camera out. This is going to be a great shot."

"Get your camera out. This is going to be a great shot."

From Elizabeth

Let's start with this. I'm afraid the word *gratitude* has grown trite in our world. It's become a meme we see on Facebook or TikTok. It's largely lost its meaning in the midst of overused platitudes, cute posters, and reflexive responses to hard times.

But as Ellie discovered on the golf course, true gratitude is the essence of wisdom. It's making peace with your situation in life and finding the good. It's about finding a deep appreciation for every extra bit we get because nothing is guaranteed. She found true gratitude that day. It was a moment of appreciation, contentment, and satisfaction.

Imagine if we intentionally cultivated this experience. Imagine if we regularly connected with our bodies, experiences, minds, spirits, and souls every day, and we did it *on purpose*. Think of the tone that would be set for our days, and how our lives would change with this deep understanding of gratitude.

Ellie was 63 when she went golfing that day. You may be younger or older than she was. Please don't wait until life teaches you this lesson. This revelation can be adopted at any age. It's something that is done on purpose. It is an integral part of wisdom, allowing us to live more fully in our HeartPrint.

Gratitude brought Ellie closer to her HeartPrint, and what happened next shows how naturally that wisdom began to guide her days. So much happened that I don't have time to share. I'm happy to let you know that Joe and Ellie continued to golf together for the next several years. They lived a connected and full life. Joe was the love of Ellie's life.

Ten years after this golf outing, almost to the day, her dear Joe passed away. It was one of the saddest days of her life. A whole book could be written about that. Joe barely got to know his granddaughter, Viv. He missed out on some of the most precious years Ellie had. Someday, I will tell you all about it.

And, in case you are wondering, Chase got married. It was a wonderful event. He married an incredible woman, and they had Ellie's granddaughter a few years later. As Viv grew up, she started calling Ellie "Grandma Bunny" because Ellie had given her the old, tattered stuffed animal from her childhood. Ellie had kept it tucked away in a box all those years, waiting for the perfect time.

In Joe's absence, Ellie grew closer to Chase and became more deeply woven into her precious Viv's life. Their Saturday breakfasts became a cherished ritual. Of course, I have so much more I could tell you, but I will save that for later. There are just a couple more stories that *must* be told.

A Cup of Tea with Meg

Deep, natural appreciation is a sign we are living in harmony with our Wise Woman and therefore our HeartPrint. Getting beyond the trite, shallow ideas surrounding gratitude can be a challenge. Hopefully, these journal prompts will help:

- What makes Ellie's gratitude different?
- How can we nurture this kind of appreciation in our lives?
- What stands in the way of experiencing this kind of gratitude?
- When was the last time you had the experience of deep gratitude? How might you expand this so you can feel it today?

Chapter 19 · Age 76

on the porch of her son's home in Trumbull, Connecticut—the circle is completed

Ellie sat alone on the porch of her son's house in a rocking chair, with a large glass of lemonade on the table next to her. Chase and his wife had moved to the outskirts of town a few years ago so their daughter could have more room to play and to live a less-cluttered life. Ellie's eyes were fixed on her 10-year-old granddaughter, Viv, playing on a dirt hill with a friend. She smiled as she heard the laughter of children lost in play. She closed her eyes and thought about Joe, who had passed away three years earlier.

"I'm sad you're missing this, Joe," she said out loud.

She watched the scene unfold. She heard Viv laugh loudly and sprint away from her friend. Viv jumped on her bicycle. "Wait up, Viv!" her friend shouted. Ignoring the pleas, Viv started peddling toward the house.

"Go fast, Viv," Ellie said quietly.

"What's that, Mom?" Chase had arrived.

"Oh, nothing," Ellie said. "Your daughter, Genevieve, likes to go fast," she said, pointing.

Chase laughed. "Yes, she does. I wonder who she gets that from?"

Viv started having trouble navigating the rough terrain coming down the hill.

"Uh-oh," Chase said.

With her friend running behind her, Viv lost control and fell off her bike, tumbling down the hill. Chase jumped off the porch to help her. Ellie started walking quickly toward the scene of the incident. By the time she arrived, Viv was crying loudly.

"You're alright, darling," Chase said. "You just messed up your knee a little."

"It's bleeding," Viv said. "It hurts."

"I know," Chase said. "Maybe Grandma Bunny can help with that."

"Carry her to the porch," Ellie said. "I'll get a bandage."

A few minutes later, Ellie was cleaning and treating the scrape on Viv's knee.

"How scary was that?" Ellie asked her granddaughter.

"Scary," Viv replied. "I thought I was going to *die*."

"That *is* scary," Ellie replied. "Tell me more."

"I was going so *fast*," Viv said. "And I tried to put on my brakes and there was a rock and then, boom!" she said, looking up at her grandmother. "I thought I was going to die," she repeated.

"Oh my," Ellie replied, wrapping the wound in a bandage. "That is scary. How did it feel?" she asked softly.

Viv thought for a moment. "I don't know," she started. "I flew off my bike and, well, then I can't remember. I almost hit the rock," she concluded.

"Yes," her grandmother said. "Very, *very* scary. What about coming down the hill, before you fell?" she asked.

"It was awesome!" Viv answered. "I love going fast."

"I love that about you," Ellie answered. "That is a part of your HeartPrint," she said, touching Viv's heart. "Never stop going fast, sweetheart," she continued. "I'll bet you'll watch out for rocks the next time."

Ellie paused from her work on Viv's knee and looked up. "I remember when I was about your age. I fell off my bike, too," she said. Ellie finished the bandage and patted Viv's leg.

"You used to ride a bike?" Viv asked as she played with the now-wrapped bandage on her knee.

"Of course!" Ellie replied. "I was the fastest kid in my school."

"You were?"

"Yup. And one day, I fell off. I got the breath knocked out of me. It was really scary."

"So, what did you do, Grandma Bunny?" Viv asked. "Did you stop going fast?"

Ellie thought back and felt sadness. "To be honest with you, Viv, yes, I did. But I wish I hadn't. I wish I had kept riding like the wind. Just like I hope you are going to do. Just be a little more careful."

Viv thought for a minute. "Okay, Grandma, I'll keep going fast. I'll just watch out for rocks," she said, looking at her grandmother for approval.

"That's my girl," Ellie said, smiling and patting Viv on the top of her head. "Now, I think dinner's ready. Will your friend be joining us?"

"Nah," Viv replied. "She had to go home."

"Okay. Well, I think your mom has dinner ready. And I brought some ice cream for dessert."

Ellie stood up. "Grandma Bunny?" Viv asked.

"Yes, dear?" Ellie answered.

"Thank you for taking care of me. It feels better now."

"Good!" Ellie replied. "Now, let's go eat."

"Never stop going fast, sweetheart."

From Elizabeth

Well, we are nearing the end of our story. I'm glad this part was included. Ellie came full circle here, from her bike to Viv's. Seven decades earlier, Ellie's mom did the best she could. She made sure her daughter was physically safe. But she couldn't help Ellie with all of her questions. If she could have, she would have, I'm sure. Now, it was Ellie's turn. It was so special that Ellie was able to provide not just the first aid for Viv's body but also the reassurance and understanding she needed to navigate the fears and doubts that came with the fall.

Ellie was still living in her HeartPrint most of the time. She still loved to journal, and most of the words on the pages listed the things she was happy about. Her *Shadow Sisters* were still bringing up things, and Ellie loved and appreciated each of them. They felt assured that they would be listened to and understood, but not given center stage.

What about the Basement of Shadows? Yes, she visited it from time to time. But mostly it was to discover the next step of her journey. Ellie had come to understand that you never get it "done," and you never get it "right." There is always an expansion of the soul waiting. There is always something to be learned.

Ellie lived most days showing up as her Wise Woman self—the unique and best version of herself. She was mostly healthy and grateful for it. She had learned to find wisdom in others. These were truly golden years filled with the joy of family and friends.

She learned to accept change and, even when she felt afraid to try new things, she trusted herself to keep expanding further into her HeartPrint. She grew to appreciate the small moments of wonder and peace that dotted each day. She freely offered her compassion and made her wisdom available, trusting others to step into it when they were ready. Small moments, like the ones she had with Viv, made life precious.

I'd like to visit with you one final time about you and your Wise Woman. I hope you can hear her voice more clearly as you read through the pages of this book. I hope she is guiding you ever closer to your HeartPrint. Like I said a long time ago, she may or may not sound like me. Your journey is *your* journey. Your pain and confusion belong uniquely to you. Your *Shadow Sisters* are a precious part of who you are.

I wish so much for you to experience a life that feels good. I wish for you to live a life that is, as much as possible, connected to your Wise Woman and aligned with your HeartPrint. I long for you to understand the agency and control you have over your happiness. It is so worth the work to get there.

Perhaps a plan is forming in your mind. Maybe you've started your own journal. Maybe you've even given your Wise Woman a name! I must give you fair warning that, like Ellie, you too will face setbacks. There will be times of discouragement. Sometimes, you will feel like a failure. That's okay.

I have one more piece of advice: Become aware of the wisdom that surrounds you. I learned over my long life that wisdom can be found in the voice of a child or in the message of a preacher. It can be discovered in an honest conversation with a dear friend or in a tense meeting with a teacher. Most of all, it can be found within. You can become the person you were meant to be.

Listen to the voice of your Wise Woman. She asks good questions. She gives good advice. Give yourself the space to honestly explore your feelings and thoughts. Accept yourself with all of your shortcomings, understanding they form the compass that will guide you ever closer to your HeartPrint.

Well, that is it. This is the last you will hear from me, in this book anyway. Ellie enjoyed another decade in this world, but we won't hear anything about those years. In this book, it's time to say goodbye.

A Cup of Tea with Meg

We are nearing the end of our journey. Ellie is living out her legacy. Here are some thoughts as you consider yours:

- How important is your legacy to you? Why?
- Who are the people who left you a legacy? What was it? What legacy do you want to leave behind?
- Are you living your life in a way that allows your legacy to live on after you?
- What changes might you like to make to bring you closer to your HeartPrint?

Chapter 20 · Age 89

on the hospital bed inside Chase's home office—the final reunion

Ellie lay on an adjustable hospital bed that had been arranged in Chase's home office. A few months earlier, Chase and his wife had insisted she come to them so they and Viv could take care of her, along with the hospice nurses. The time for her departure drew near.

Ellie slowly opened her eyes. As sometimes happens when waking from a dream, she wasn't sure where she was or what time it was. Although her eyesight was failing, she looked around the room, trying to orient herself. She noticed both of her hands were being held. The other hands were familiar. "Joe, is that you?" she muttered.

"No, Mom, it's me, Chase," her son said quietly, not wanting to remind her that Joe had passed away years earlier. "We're all here."

Gathered around Ellie's bed were Chase, his wife, and Viv, their daughter. They were joined by Grace, her best friend, and Ree, her friend from the community garden. They had come, not knowing if they would get a chance to speak to Ellie or not. The nurse had told them that the end was near.

Viv stepped forward and stood next to her father. "Hi, Grandma Bunny."

"Viv?" Ellie said, "Is that you?"

"Yes, Grandma, it's me, Viv. I love you," she said through her tears.

"I love you, too," Ellie said. "I'm confused," she continued, still trying to get her bearings.

"We thought we'd lost you," Chase said. "It was touch and go for a while."

Ellie sighed. "Well, it's nice to be home," she said. "Where's Joe?"

No one answered.

Grace walked to the other side of the bed. "Hi, Elles!"

"Oh, my dear Grace," Ellie said affectionately. "Come closer."

Grace leaned over the bed and came so close their foreheads touched. "It's been fun," Grace said, smiling.

"Yes, we've had a nice run," Ellie said quietly as she gained awareness. "I'm so glad to see you. I love you with all my heart. Is this it?"

"Maybe so," Grace said. "I love you."

It was quiet for a few minutes as those who loved Ellie stood around the bed, cherishing the few moments they had left with her.

Then, inside, Ellie felt a sudden surge of energy. "Oh!" she said in a louder voice. "James! It's so good to see you, brother."

Once again, no one wanted to say that her brother had died five years earlier.

The silence was broken by Viv, who was still crying. "Grandma Bunny?" she said.

Ellie recognized from her tone of voice that she had something very important to discuss. "Can I speak to my granddaughter alone for a minute?" she asked clearly. Her energy was growing.

The room emptied. "Now, tell Grandma Bunny what's on your mind," Ellie said, taking Viv's hands in hers.

"Well," she started slowly. "I just don't know what I'm going to do without you." Viv was weeping. "What am I going to do without our Saturday breakfasts?" Viv continued. "And who am I going to talk to about my mom and dad? And I don't even know if I want to go to college. And I don't want you to go. Please don't go."

Chapter 20 • Age 89

Ellie held Viv's head to her chest. "Go ahead, sweetheart, I know. I know."

Time passed with only the sound of Viv sobbing.

"I know it's scary," Ellie finally said. "I'm a little scared, too. But know this in your heart of hearts: We have shared love. And that's something that lasts forever. No one can take that away from us. I know there will come a time when you'll give the same love to your children and your grandchildren. I promise you there will be many others you'll love. And they will love you back. But nothing will ever replace what we've shared together. Keep your heart open, my dearest. There's room for a lot more love in there."

Viv stood up, and their eyes met.

"You're so much wiser than I was at your age," Ellie said. "Your mom and dad love you so *much*. You have a whole life to live. And you must *pay attention*. Life has a way of showing you the way to go.

"You see, Viv darling, I'm about to shift into another form. My body may not be here, but I will always be in your heart. We will always have a thread of connection. Find that thread inside you and call on me. You'll see me and feel me. I promise I will be with you forever. You'll find me in the way you live your life. You'll hear my voice as you live your own life, and become a mother and grandmother."

Then, Ellie squeezed Viv's hand firmly. "And don't forget about the books on my shelf," she said with conviction.

Viv didn't understand the last part. She wiped her face. Before she could ask a question about it, Ellie said, "Now, go tell Joe and James I want to see them."

"But Grandma," Viv started, then stopped herself. "Okay, I'll go tell them," she said as she walked out of the room, leaving Ellie alone.

Ellie closed her eyes. When she opened them again, everyone was there.

"There you are!" Ellie was certain she recognized the voice. It was her old friend, Elizabeth. "It's time to go," Elizabeth said firmly. "Come on, I have lots to show you. You can say your goodbyes now."

Ellie felt another surge of energy. She sat up straight and turned, dangling her feet over the side of the bed. She climbed out and stood up with surprising ease. It was effortless. Her family was still standing around. She slowly walked around and affectionately touched each of them. She put her hand on Chase's shoulder. She touched Grace's face. She hugged Viv, kissing her softly on the cheek. They were all crying and didn't seem to notice her affection.

"She gave us so much," Chase's wife said.

"I can't believe she's gone," Chase said.

"She was the best friend I've ever had," Grace said.

"It feels like she's still here," Viv said. "Grandma Bunny …"

Then Ellie looked at the bed. She saw herself there, motionless.

Then she noticed she was wearing jeans and a sweater. She looked at her feet and saw some very familiar hiking boots.

Realizing what had happened, she thought, *I'll miss them all.*

Next, she felt a familiar hand in hers. It was Elizabeth. "You're leaving behind something very special," she said. "But it's time for us to move on."

Hand in hand, they began to walk out of the room. Slowly, magically, Ellie and Elizabeth merged into one person. Next, each of her *Shadow Sisters* joined them. They were quiet and respectful. At long last, they all shared the same thoughts, the same words, and the same feelings.

Then she heard another voice. "Ellie?"

"Joe?" she asked. "Where have you been?"

"Waiting for you," Joe said.

Ellie started walking toward the voice.

Then she heard a different voice. "Hey, sis!" It was James.

"James!" she said excitedly and hugged him. "C'mon," James said, "Joe's waiting for us."

James and Ellie took a few more steps and saw Joe. After a warm embrace, Joe said, "Ellie, do I have some stories to tell you …"

Joe and Ellie walked arm in arm with James next to them. They talked excitedly, with occasional bursts of warm laughter. It was time to enter the next chapter of their existence.

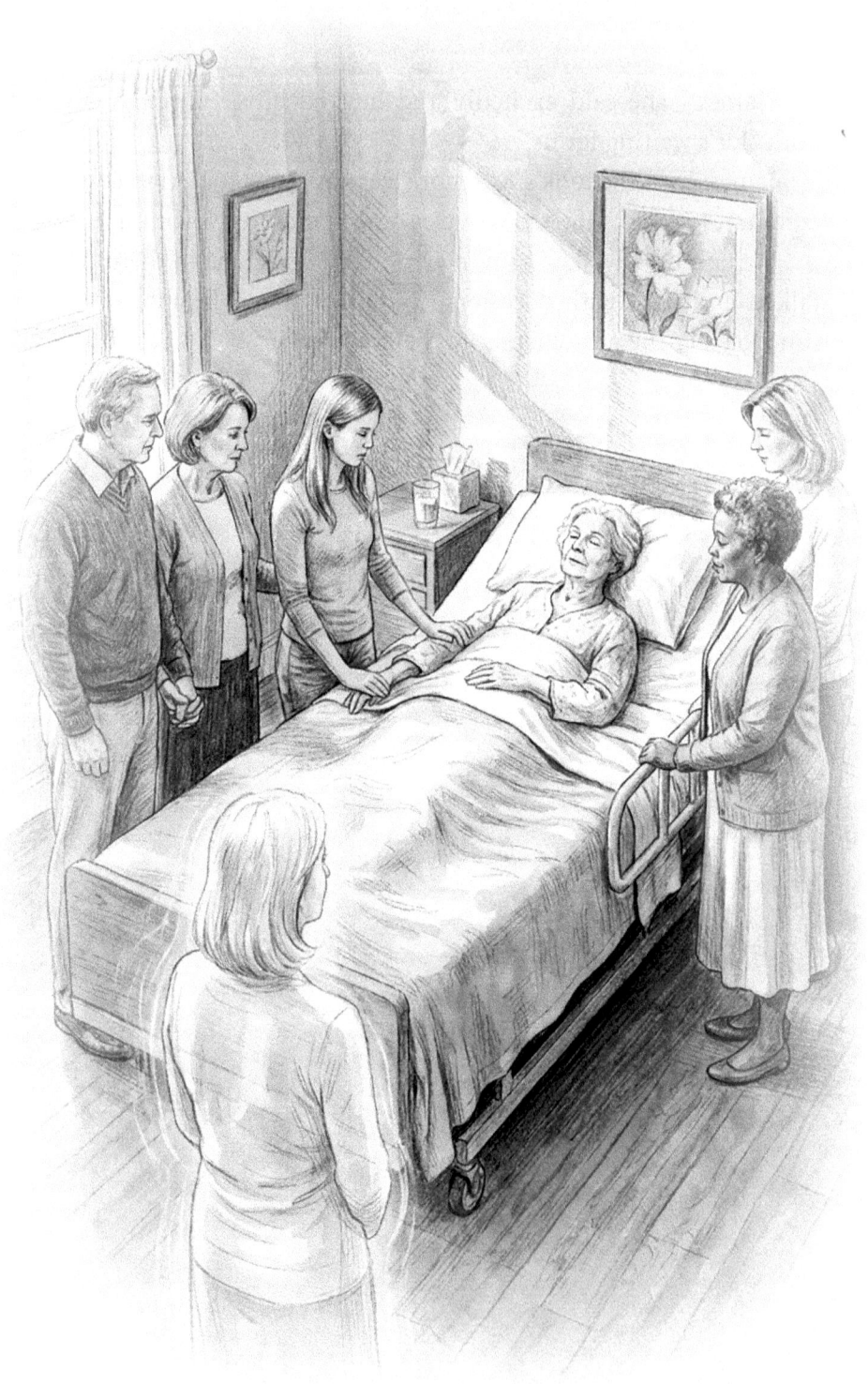

Then Ellie looked at the bed. She saw herself there, motionless.

Epilogue

outside of Paradise Funeral Home on a sacred bench before Grandma Bunny's service—the story continues

On the day of Grandma Bunny's funeral, Viv was going for a walk in the garden next to the funeral home before the service began. She was distracted, confused, and sad. She needed to walk before facing what was ahead.

"It's a beautiful day, isn't it?"

When Viv heard the question, she turned and saw an older woman sitting on a bench. She hadn't noticed her before.

"Yes, it's nice," Viv said politely.

"Something is bothering you, child," the woman said kindly. "I'll bet it's about something in there," she said, nodding her head toward the funeral home.

"No, it's nothing," Viv replied patiently. She turned away.

"I can remember what it's like to say goodbye to someone you love. I can see it in your face. Tell me about it," the woman persisted, patting the seat next to her on the bench.

Viv turned toward her and saw a warm smile. It reminded her of Grandma Bunny—of Ellie. "Well, I just lost my grandmother," she said, still standing.

"Oh my," the woman said. "Were you close?"

Viv hesitated. She took a big breath and said, "Well, that's the thing. I could always talk to her about … things."

There was silence.

"Yes, it does help to talk about … *things*," the woman said.

Viv took a step closer to the bench. "I'm trying to decide whether to stay here for college or move to Pennsylvania," she said, looking into the woman's eyes, her eyes welling with tears.

"Big decision," the woman replied. "That must be tough."

That simple response gave Viv permission to continue. "My boyfriend and parents want me to stay here. But my friend and I have always planned to go away to college together."

Viv walked over and slowly sat down next to the woman. The familiar story was recurring, once by a creek and now in a garden.

"I'm Genevieve," the woman said, changing the subject. Viv couldn't put words to it, but she felt her HeartPrint glow for the first time in a while.

"Genevieve?" Viv asked. "That's amazing," she said. "I'm Viv. It's short for Genevieve."

The woman smiled warmly.

Viv instinctively started sharing all she was going through. Genevieve would ask questions, sigh, and laugh at all the right times.

The conversation was interrupted by the sound of ringing bells. Viv looked at the clock on her phone. "I have to go back in there. It's time for the service to start. Thank you for listening to me. Really."

Genevieve smiled and said, "Who knows, maybe we'll meet again sometime."

"I'd like that," Viv replied. "Thank you again." Viv stood up from the bench and walked toward the funeral home. She noticed she felt lighter. She began to think about her move to Pennsylvania and how to talk to her parents and boyfriend about it. Viv didn't turn around, but if she had, she would have seen only a wisp of vapor where Genevieve had sat.

A while later, Viv and her father, Chase, went to what had been Ellie's home for the past three decades. It was time to do what happens after someone passes. Their plan was to sort through Ellie's possessions and decide what to do with them. Viv was both apprehensive and expectant as they drove to the house. She longed to be close to her Grandma Bunny's presence, but the idea of going into a home that had been so full of life for so long and finding only silence was troubling.

Her spirit changed the moment she walked through the door. The first thing she noticed was the sweet fragrance that was uniquely her grandmother's. It was a papery soft, faint smell of roses. Viv's anxiety was replaced with connection and warmth.

She and her father walked together through the rooms without saying anything. Chase touched a photo of himself and Hugo the tortoise that was hanging on the wall. Viv sat down at the kitchen table, where she and Ellie had shared many Saturday mornings over breakfast. She remembered Grandma Bunny had been the one to first introduce her to tea. The teapot and cups had come to represent genuine conversation, light laughter, and earnest advice.

"I'll get started in the basement," Chase finally said. "Why don't you check out the bookshelf?" he continued, recalling Ellie's instruction that Viv sort through her library when this time came.

Viv sauntered slowly into the study and began to remove the books, placing them in a box. She remembered what Grandma Bunny had said in their last conversation about not forgetting the books.

After the first few, she noticed several books that didn't have titles on their spines. They were all arranged in a row next to one another. She pulled out the first one and saw the word "Reflections" inscribed on the front cover. She opened it and saw her grandmother's writing.

She sat on the couch nearby and started thumbing through the pages. She was captivated by the notes and sketches she found. She realized these must be the journals her grandmother had talked about from time to time. Viv caught a glimpse of her grandmother's journey. She saw deeply personal revelations on each page. She ran her finger over lists of steps her grandmother had made. *Wow, Grandma Bunny went through a lot,* she thought.

She returned to the bookshelf and ran her fingers along the spines of each book until she reached the final one. She stood there and opened it. There, on the first page, she saw this:

My Dearest Viv,

I know how much you love books. And I guessed you would be drawn to these. If you are reading this, I'm probably gone.

Tears welled up. Viv brushed them away with a sigh and kept reading.

I want you to have these journals. They are my gift to you. If you decide to read them, you will see me a bit differently than you have before. I've not always been "Grandma Bunny." I want to share my journey with you.

I hope you become friends with your Wise Woman and live in your HeartPrint. It's who you're meant to be. I hope if you can read about what I have gone through and see my struggles, it will help you with yours. You are such a strong and special person. Your mom and dad have gotten you off to a good start. I'm so thankful for that. But your life is yours and yours alone. I want you to live it with everything you have.

By the way, if you go back to the bookshelf, you'll find a pen. It was my favorite. I want you to have it.

The rest of these pages are blank. They are for you to fill with your thoughts, feelings, plans, and dreams. Happy writing!

I love you and I am always with you.

Love,
Grandma Bunny

Then, on the next page, there was a drawing that Viv would cherish for the rest of her life. She ran her fingers over it, tracing the different parts of it. As her finger touched the page, something magical happened. A small gold ribbon of light, flexing and twisting, came off the page. It swirled around Viv, dancing in the air, as if it were looking for a place to land.

Then, with purpose, it went straight into Viv's heart, disappearing with a small swooshing sound. Viv closed her eyes and saw herself and Grandma Bunny, arms linked, walking together across Viv's long and wonderful life. Then, she saw another, different woman walking with them. Viv wasn't sure, but it looked a lot like Genevieve.

The familiar story was recurring, once by a creek and now in a garden.

"A ribbon of light connecting one heart to another across space and time."

Acknowledgments

This book has taken me a long time to write—five years to the month, in fact. It was originally going to be a workbook, and I quickly found that while I can write programs, trainings, and events, I am far less skilled in the writing you find in this book. Bob Harpole was the fourth ghostwriter I tried over the course of three years. It is because of him this story exists the way it does. I will be forever grateful for the stars and constellations that aligned to allow us to meet and work together. We met every Friday for more than two years, and this gentle, accepting friendship definitively changed my life. Bob, I love you so. Thank you for walking beside me on this journey and helping me bring to life this complicated structure of a book. Part memoir, part story, and part self-help.

Every idea I brought you—even when we had somewhat "finished" the book—you would ponder over and then feel the truth that Elizabeth needed this new idea woven in. Despite the extra work, you took the care to weave it in, in that wonderful way you do.

For my team at Making Relationships Work, past or present, whether you're in Operations, a Coach, a Clinician, or perhaps you have a role that is in between all of these things, I am grateful for you every day. Thank you for believing in me, for walking with me, for stretching with me, and for your kind and good humor. Our clients receive the very best care in the world because of you. I am so thankful for our community.

For my clients, many of your stories are threaded throughout this book. Twisted together, woven, and representing many of the facets of what it is to be a woman doing the work. I love each and every one of you, and I feel the weight and privilege of being a part of your journey.

Next, I'd like to mention my mentors, therapists, friends, family, advocates, and cheer squad, many of whom I have partnered with over the years to walk my own path of healing and returning home to my Wise Woman and my HeartPrint. Your generous teaching, giving me a safe place to heal and grow, has provided me with the scaffolding to rebuild myself from the ashes of crisis to here. Thank you immensely. I love and appreciate you more than words can say. You have inspired my work and my mission to serve women and families. I love you.

Finally, for my own family. My husband, Alfred, and two incredible sons, Tex and Xander. To my sister, Ri, and her daughter, Ru. I love you all infinitely. Thank you for being my home—a place where I belong completely, and where I am seen and understood. A place where you want to understand when you don't. Where my gifts, talents, failures, foibles, and quirks are celebrated and accepted without question. I am the luckiest.

Continue the conversation.

Find reflections, resources, and companion content at

megantuohey.com/book

@megtuoheyofficial

Megan Tuohey - Making Relationships Work

@megtuoheyofficial

@megtuoheyofficial

The Wisdom Stripes Podcast

megantuohey.com/wisdom-stripes

About the Author

Meg Tuohey is a licensed psychologist, relationship expert, and founder of Making Relationships Work, a pioneering company that has helped more than 4,000 women and couples repair relationships through her evidence-based methodology. Known for blending rigorous clinical practice with compassion, her work empowers women to rebuild self-trust, navigate crisis, and lead their lives with clarity and strength, especially when traditional approaches have failed.

In Meg's first book, HeartPrint, she brings her deeply compassionate voice and human insight to the page, inviting women everywhere to return to the wisdom already inside them.

Meg lives with her husband and business partner, Alfred, and the family they built together — a life shaped by resilience, purpose, and her lifelong commitment to helping women reclaim their power.

www.ingramcontent.com/pod-product-compliance
Lightning Source LLC
Chambersburg PA
CBHW070615030426
42337CB00020B/3809